BERNIES ABOUT

NORTH EAST

Bernie Slaven's
Unedited
Interviews

First published in Great Britain by 7 Enterprises Ltd

ISBN no 978-0-9560684-2-2

Cover design by Graeme Bandeira

Printed in Singapore by Tien Wah Press.

ACKNOWLEDGEMENTS..............

I would like to thank the managers and players for giving their time,each and every one of them a character.

A massive thanks yet again to Graeme Bandeira for the best art work yet.

Adam Steel for his patience and help as proof reader, without him the book would be unreadable.Also the North East reporters who thought of the questions for my interview.

Thanks to Clarrissa for making the book possible.

Also thanks to Eddie and everyone at studio print in Redcar for doing the final touches.

Thanks also to Real Radio for allowing me to use the Sir Bobby interview and giving the book a plug on the airwaves.

Peter and Barry at Hillstreet Center Middlesbrough and Jo at Debenhams Metro Centre for letting me sign and sell the book in the stores.

ALSO AVAILABLE FROM 7 ENTERPRISES

BERNIES ABOUT

Interviews with past Boro stars, Charlton,Clough, Gascoigne,Hardwick,Johnstone, Juninho,Mannion,Merson, Murdoch, Ravanelli,Rioch,Robson, Souness, Stiles and guest celebrity Chis Rea.

BERNIES ABOUT 2

Interviews with past Boro stars,Allison,Armstrong, Boam, Branca, Downing,Emerson, Ince, Mills, Mowbray, Neal, Pallister, Ugolini, Viduka,Wheater.

Available at www.bernieslaven.co.uk

Email seven.enterprises@hotmail.co.uk

DEDICATION..............

I would like to dedicate this book to my ex team mate Gary
Parkinson. Gary suffered a stroke back in September 2010. He
has been left with a condition know as 'locked in syndrome'.
I first met Gary, when I joined Middlesbrough back in 1984/85
season. I liked him instantly.He was born and bred in Thornaby,
just outside of Middlesbrough. He wore the Boro shirt with
pride,was an all round good defender,who possessed a fantastic
shot. One of his goals that lives in my memory, is when we
played Everton at Goodison in a FA Cup tie and Parky hit a
35yard top corner, beating one of the best keepers around
Neville Southall. Parky used to take penalty kicks as well and in
the premier league the first season we played Ipswich Town at
Ayresome park, myself and Parky argued for the ball. I won the
argument and missed the penalty. When we returned to the
dressing room, I turned to Parky and said' I told you, you should
have taken it.' he just laughed. Off the park he was a clean living
lad who fancied himself as a bit of a singer. The biggest
compliment I can pay him is, if you had a daughter, you would
want her to marry someone like Parky.
He married his childhood sweetheart Debbie and they now have
two daughters and a son.
Our thoughts and prayers are with the family at this difficult
time and we hope Parky can keep fighting and overcome his
condition.
Thanks for buying the book in doing so you are helping him and
his family.

£1.00 from every book sold will go to the Gary Parkinson
fund.If anyone wants to donate more you can go on his website
and make a donation.

www.garyparky.co.uk

"The difficulties you meet will resolve themselves as you advance,proceed and light will dawn, and shine with increasing clearness on your path."

INTRODUCTION ....

The Bernies About idea came when I worked for Boro TV
between 1998-2002.
Over those years I met some of the greatest players ever to wear
the red shirt of Middlesbrough as well as some high profile
managers. The job involved traveling up and down the country
accompanied by a camera man. I met players at hotels, in the
comfort of their own homes at training grounds and even on
boats. Over a period of time I interviewed over 200 players,
managers and personalities. And throughly enjoyed speaking to
every one of them.
Some were clever, outspoken, outrageous, opinionated, quiet,
eccentric, charming, smug and even arrogant, but everyone was
an individual and to their credit none of them asked me for a fee.
They gave up their free time and answered my questions openly
and honestly.

It was an honour and a privilege to interview World Cup
Winners, European Cup Winners, people who have been
successful in their profession.

After a great success with my two first books I decided to write
a North East version. I interviewed some North East Legends to
put alongside my Boro
Interviews.
I hope you enjoy these interviews and get an insight into what
the players are actually like on and off the field and what makes
them tick.

CONTENTS

MIDDLESBROUGH

NEWCASTLE

SUNDERLAND

"I was certainly brave, because I was thick enough and young enough not to know about fear. Only intelligent people know about fear."

Describing his style as a centre forward.

BRIAN CLOUGH
MIDDLESBROUGH

BRIAN
CLOUGH

Cloughie was born in Grove hill Middlesbrough on 21st March 1935. He became a full time professional at his home town club in May 1952 and made his league debut in September 1955, against Barnsley. In total Cloughie made 222 appearances for Boro scoring a phenomenal 204 goals.

I travelled to Nottingham to meet Cloughie. At the time Brian's house was been renovated, that was old big heads excuse anyway, so we met up with him at his big mates home a guy called Colin Lawrence to do the interview. When Brian arrived he shook everyone's hands then nestled down in his seat, as we had a pre chat, he turned to my mate who weighs twenty eight stone and asked are you from the boro then. Next question was what school did my mate go to, then boy you must have ate some school dinners. Everyone in the room burst out laughing.

Cloughie was everything I expected, controversial, opinionated, outspoken, charming, before the chat I asked,would you like me to go through the questions with you, carry on young man was his well documented catch phrase.

Looking at the past and present goals scorers over the years at Middlesbrough Cloughie without doubt is the greatest to wear the red shirt of his home town club .

He retired from football management in 1993 and sadly passed away on the 20th September 2004.

I was honoured and privileged to meet one of the games most charismatic and successful figures.

BERNIE

You were born and bred in Middlesbrough - what was it like growing up in the Boro?

CLOUGHIE

Well, I was very happy Bernie, extremely happy. I fell into football because I was thick academically, as you've already established this morning! I was extremely happy, born and bred in Valley Road, near Albert Park.

I was obsessed with sport even when I was a little child, neglected school obviously like a lot of us did in those days, and I was very, very happy. We used to live next door to the Steelworks football club and they had a cricket pitch also and I was a fanatical cricket fan. It was cricket obviously during the summer - when we got a summer in Middlesbrough. We didn't get a lot of sun in Middlesbrough. It makes me laugh when all these foreign players come up to Middlesbrough, you know, and after about six months the wives say they can't stand the weather. I turn to my wife Barbara and I say: 'You know, I never saw one palm tree in Middlesbrough while I lived there for 20-odd years.' I never saw a bloody coconut until I went abroad, and the players' wives say they can't stand the weather. What the hell does she think it is in Middlesbrough, bloody sunshine like Florida? Anyway, Clairville, Steelworks Club, and Albert Park, that was my three.

When I eventually signed for Middlesbrough, I used to walk through Albert Park but inevitably I was late so I used to run through and walk back afterwards.

BERNIE

Who were your boyhood heroes?

CLOUGHIE

Well, it was the whole of the Middlesbrough side. They were full of heroes you know, Middlesbrough Football Club, considering we won nowt. We had the Wilf Mannions, the

Mickey Fentons, I followed Mickey Fenton into the side, George Camsell and Alex McCrae, who was one of your lot.

BERNIE

I'm Irish!

CLOUGHIE

You're Irish are you? You don't sound it! There was Jimmy Gordon, who worked with me for many years afterwards, Harry Bell who played wing half. They kept floating out all these so it wasn't just one particular hero, we had a lot. We had a bloke called Blenkinsopp, who was rumoured to have only played when he'd had a couple of pints before the match!
It was all rumours, but he certainly had one after the match I know that! Dicky Robinson, he played, and he got in with the England side eventually.
They were good players and they were regarded as a very exciting side but, as a I say, we won nowt.

BERNIE

You played football for Billingham Synthonia and Great Broughton. Who was it that spotted you?

CLOUGHIE

Well, I went to Great Broughton, which is a village just outside Middlesbrough, and I went through my brothers. I played with the four of my brothers at Great Broughton when I was 15 or 16. I played for Billingham Synthiona because I worked at ICI.

BERNIE

I played for them last year.

CLOUGHIE

You look older! I played for Billingham Synthonia, one of the first clubs I got a few bob from. In those days you used to play three nights at the end of the season, and I got a few bob from Billingham for expenses, more than I was getting working for ICI. I was a messenger boy at the ICI, and I played for South Bank and got a few bob from South Bank. But Great Broughton was the initial thing, and of course my brother was several years older than me. Our Des was older than me, Billy was older than me and I was the fourth in line. I got in the side when I was about 16 I think.

BERNIE

Who was it that actually spotted you?

CLOUGHIE

To get up there it was just family connections, it was just about 'you're ready, you can come up'. We used to go up on a potato lorry, in the back. Sanderson's had a firm.

BERNIE

I think I saw that last week.

CLOUGHIE

You would have done - it will be the same lorry as well. He would deliver his stuff into Middlesbrough, and then he'd pick us up at lunch time and take us to Broughton. We'd go into a pub and play darts until it was two o'clock, until they got the sheep off the field. Because there was bloody sheep on the pitch and they had to clear the sheep off before we could start, and I enjoyed it. The women who used to run it ran the post office at Great Broughton. They called her Nancy Goldsmith. That's a long time ago.

BERNIE

Four years after joining Boro you made your first team debut against Barnsley. Do you remember anything about that?

CLOUGHIE

I remember the guy I played against - Harry Hough they called him. Blondish, going bald, wing half. I remember playing there. I think we lost. I remember the immortal words that Bob Dennison, the manager, said to me as we were walking out of the tunnel, out of the dressing room to the tunnel.
It was a real booster to me. He said: 'Well, it's up to you now', and when he said that to me it was a real booster. There I was going out on my debut. I'd had a pretty good time at Middlesbrough reserves, but I was still fourth choice and then eventually I wound my way through and got in against Barnsley and we lost. But I stayed in the team and then went out again.

BERNIE

People described you as a brave, confident, ruthless, centre forward. How would you describe yourself?

CLOUGHIE

Well, I was certainly brave because I was thick enough and young enough not to know about fear. Only intelligent people know about fear. You know, older people say to me all the young men that used to fly aeroplanes during the war, they weren't thick but they didn't know about fear. But once you know about fear you are frightened and if you tend to think about your job, you get frightened on occasions.

But I wasn't frightened. I used to take the centre halves on as part and parcel of my job, you know, despite the fact that they were kicking me for three quarters of the game. I used to take them on as an equal and I had a knack. I can't explain why I scored more goals than anybody else.

I knew I liked scoring, and some of the criticism I got was from my mates at Ayresome Park. They'd say the only time I would talk is during the match, and all you shout is 'pull it back' so you can score. I said: 'Well, who's the best goalscorer in this team?' They would say: 'You get your forties, like.'

I said: 'Well, I'm the best so you might as well give it to me.' I played with a lad called Ronnie Burbeck, who played outside left. He brought that up in a team talk. He said: 'He's always shouting for the ball boss when he gets near the penalty area.' I said: 'Well, I'll tell you what. The next time I shout and you ignore me, go and put it in.' I think he only got four goals a season.

BERNIE

You spent seven seasons at Ayresome Park. Did it frustrate you that you never actually played in the top flight?

CLOUGHIE

Yes, it frustrated me personally, because I was in the goals and I was scoring enough goals for two teams to get promotion. I know there was a lot of goals in those days, more than there is now in modern day football, but when your getting forties as I was getting - I was getting, 38, 39, 40, 41.

BERNIE

Was there a goalkeeper in those days!?

CLOUGHIE

Aye, there was goalkeepers. I used to stick them through Sam Bartram's legs. He used to play for Charlton. But I was in the brackets of over 40. You see, to score all that many goals and not win something, it was ridiculous.
There were sides getting promoted every season in the second division scoring half the goals we were scoring, but we couldn't keep a clean sheet to save our lives. And that stood me in good stead when I went into management, because my first priority when I went into management was to keep a clean sheet and I built on that. I built every team I've ever managed on a clean sheet. I bought Peter Shilton, he nearly bankrupted me.
I bought him for £300.000 and his wages were astronomical even in those days. Somebody said: 'What have you bought Shilton for?' I said: 'Well, he doesn't exactly score goals but he saves 15 a year and that's 15 points to me.' And, of course, he did. He was an amazing goalkeeper. He did nowt for 89 minutes and even in the European cups that we were winning in those days, he'd do nothing, nothing , nothing, then somebody would let fly at him from 25 yards and he'd get his fingers to it. And he'd walk off and he wouldn't be dirty or anything, but that one save would have saved us the match. Incredible player. Then I

used to be obsessed with centre halves because I used to work with a lad called Peter Taylor, who was a player at Middlesbrough. Bob Dennison bought him from Coventry and I became friendly with Peter at Middlesbrough and the relationship lasted right through our careers, until he went to Derby and I stayed and all that type of thing. I was obsessed with centre halves and goalkeepers and he was obsessed with goalkeepers because he was one. I formed my opinions in management when I first started. I'd get myself a goalkeeper, I'd get myself a centre half and then I'd get myself a centre forward to sneak a goal. And if you look at my career that's what I did do. It sounds easy but it wasn't that easy.

BERNIE

You scored 204 goals in 222 appearances. How did you do it? Was it anticipation was it greed?

CLOUGHIE

It certainly wasn't luck, and I don't mean that conceitedly, because you can't get lucky 40 times a year. You can get lucky five times but not 40. Somebody once said to me when I was manager of Derby County, they said: 'Oh, you were lucky to win the league' when we beat Leeds. You can't get lucky over a season to win the league. You can get lucky over one match or two matches. But when you play 40-odd games, you can't get lucky every match and I got annoyed. When I went to Derby of course, I was still young enough to play football and I was playing a testimonial for a lad called Edwin Holliday, who used to play outside left for Middlesbrough, and he was at Peterborough. I went to play in a testimonial and I was manager of Derby and I picked meself - well, that's a good start when you're the manager! So I picked meself and we won 1-0. I scored the goal, it bobbled in the far corner. We had a Welshman playing with us called Alan Durban, he finished up managing Sunderland actually. After the match he said: 'Is that how you got all your goals?' I said: 'Aye, about 90 per cent of them. Bobbling in luckily, you know off my backside off my chin, off me eyes. If I could put them in with me ear I would!' I said I used to catch them in the middle on occasion and they used to go in. I said it was 90 per cent of 40 every season that bobble in and that shut him up. The box is where the penalty area is and that's were the posts are. I said the only thing that doesn't move on the football pitch is the posts.

BERNIE

Some of your players and fellow professionals describe you as big-headed and arrogant.

CLOUGHIE

I was certainly arrogant and I was certainly conceited to the strength of my own ability.But it wasn't a bit of arrogance, it was just that when you know what you can do.I suppose that is arrogance. I suppose because it came after a couple of years, you've only got to score 40 goals a couple of seasons running and you're bound to know after that that you can score goals. So if that's arrogance, yes I was arrogant. I had done my national service and I didn't get married early. I didn't get married until I was 24, which was late in those days you know. You used to get married when you were doing your national service. The first one you knocked off wherever you were stationed you married.

BERNIE

You had experience of that more than I did.

CLOUGHIE

I waited and then I was lucky. I fell on my feet, or my wife fell on her feet actually! We met in Rea's café along from Ayersome Park, where I used to spend some of the best hours of my life, drinking milkshakes. I met Chris Rea, the singer. I don't know whether you're interested here, but Chris Rea is a good singer and I met his family there because they used to run the Rea's café, and I'm certain I've clipped young Chris many a time. Because you used to clip anybody that got in the way, it was a way of life in Middlesbrough. Anybody smaller than you got a clip - I got my fair share, that's why I've got big ears now! I met Barbara there and we went on from there.

BERNIE

While captain of Middlesbrough, nine of your so-called teammates signed a petition for the captaincy to be taken away from you. Did you feel betrayed?

CLOUGHIE

Oh yes, I certainly did. Brian Phillips was the centre half in those days.
We bought him somewhere and he said he thought he could do the captaincy as well as me. I said: 'If you can then get it done', like, you know? And we were all on no money those days and I wasn't too happy with the way things were going. I felt we could be winning matches that we weren't winning. Of course, I then made a stand and left Middlesbrough. I didn't really want to leave them you know, I was born and bred in Middlesbrough. Once you're born in Middlesbrough you don't want to leave, you know? And especially as I had gone up through the ranks. Anyway, I set my stall out and said I was leaving the club because there's something the matter with it. And of course

eventually when I did leave, and I went to Sunderland, I was regarded as a traitor in many areas of Middlesbrough. I still lived in Middlesbrough for a period of time, then I moved to Sunderland when I got married, or after I got married.

But it wasn't: 'Aye up Cloughie, how are you, you're at Sunderland.'

It was terrible. It was only up the road Sunderland but they never forgave me.

BERNIE

Have you got one abiding memory of Ayresome Park, one that sticks in your mind?

CLOUGHIE

When there was trouble on at the time, we played Bristol I remember. We won and I stuck a hat-trick in and Len Shackleton came to me after the match because he'd finished playing and was working for a newspaper in those days. He said: 'Well, I've seen some good hat-tricks but that's as good as I've seen.' And of course I played for the Football League, I got a couple of caps while playing for Middlesbrough. There weren't tons of memories, but it was just a continuous roller coaster in the sense that I was just on it and I never got off it. And being Middlesbrough born and bred you knew everybody. I used to walk through the park, as I've told you, to go training or run. And the keepers of the park, the gardeners, I used to say to them about October when they used to change the beds of flowers: 'Hey, when's your wall flowers coming?' They used to say: 'We'll let you know Cloughie when they come.' I would be going through one morning, and he would say: 'I've got your wall flowers.' He used to have them in a wheelbarrow.

He didn't charge me or nowt like that, there was no money changed hands. Hell, no money changed hands for 25 years in my life. You used to get on the buses for nowt. They used to let me on the buses when I got on a bit, not to your level, but I got on a bit at Middlesbrough. And I used to get the occasional cake for nowt from Sparks, and I used to get my milkshakes and she gave me a Cornetto as I was going out the door once for nowt, and that was me getting on. They're on bloody 30,000 quid a week now, but I used to get me wallflowers in the barrow and it was just that kind of place, simple as that. I used to run up to the Palladium, go to the butcher's shop and the chairman of the picture house at the palladium building, was the chairman of the football club. They called him Steve Gibson, and he used to come down Valley Road in his great big bloody car, and me ma would either be cutting the privet, it was my turn to cut the privet when I got to 10.

I started cutting the bloody privet, be sweeping the bloody paths or scrubbing the steps and Gibson used to go past and. He used to give us the bloody royal wave,in this bloody big car and of course we didn't have a car.

I never had a car until I was 25 or 26, and he used to come down on his way to the ground. He used to call in the buildings up there. He had the picture house and various shops and he was the chairman of the club.

BERNIE

You earned two full England caps. Should it have been more?

CLOUGHIE

I was disappointed with Walter Winterbottom. He was in charge those days and I regarded him as an amateur. He stayed in charge of England for a long, long time. I got capped at Wembley against Sweden, we lost the first time. And I got capped at Cardiff, against Wales obviously, and I had just scored four goals the previous week or fortnight against the Welsh centre half, a lad called Mel Nurse. I stuck four past him and they were all expecting another four in the international. I never got a bloody kick, and we drew 1-1. I was rooming with Jimmy Greaves, and Jim had either just got married or was on his way to getting married, because his misses was out there and it was pouring down. She was like a bloody drowned rat standing in the rain, because we all used to stand in the bloody rain in those days. And if we could get our wives a ticket even for England it was brilliant just to get them in for nowt.

BERNIE

On the subject of England, why have you never managed your country. I asked Jack Charlton the same question?

CLOUGHIE

Well, I thought I had got it. I went down for an interview. Jack was on the short list actually. I think there was him, he went down, I went down and Lawrie McMenemy went down. There was three of us for interviews. Once again, this might sound conceited, but you know when you do a good interview. You know they used to ask you how you felt coming off having scored three goals. You knew when you played well and when you didn't. Nobody knew better than you. You know yourself when you've been good or bad or indifferent, and I had done a good interview at Lancaster Gate.

I went back to the hotel where some friends were waiting for me, and I said if it goes on interviews I've got the job. Because I doddled the interview. Anyway, they finished up giving me the England youth side, and they didn't give Jack the job either and he was qualified to get it. They didn't give Lawrie it and he was qualified. They gave Ron Greenwood it and he wasn't even on the shortlist I don't think. I think they had just settled for his type and his image. Ron Greenwood was a charming man like

Walter Winterbottom, but they weren't our type of manager. And the reason I give now, I still give to this day as I'm talking to you, I didn't get the job because I think the Football Association suspected that I was going to take over the Football Association.

BERNIE

You probably would have.

CLOUGHIE

Absolutely, certainly. I would have closed half the offices down for a start. I'd have the team first on the aeroplane in the front seats, not in the back, because all the bloody FA wallers used to go and they used to have the big cigars, the gin and tonic and the smoked salmon and we were nowt.
Even before I started playing for Middlesbrough, me dad's favourite player was Wilf Mannion and Wilf played for England. They went to Scotland, and Billy Liddell used to play for Liverpool. I think he broke Wilf's jaw. They didn't set it at the hospital and Wilf came back the next day stood in the bloody corridor of the train, couldn't get a seat and with this broken jaw. That's how they used to treat footballers and Wilf was the best inside forward. He was playing for England, he was a god here along with George Hardwick. They were gods in Middlesbrough they were.

BERNIE

How difficult was your decision to join Boro's North Eat rivals Sunderland?

CLOUGHIE

It was a difficult decision because I never wanted to leave Middlesbrough obviously. I was born and bred in Middlesbrough and was part of the furniture. To go to Sunderland was kind of being a traitor to the Middlesbrough fans, and I was very, very happy at Middlesbrough - simple as that. But I'd been on holiday and I'd signed up for a cruise and I went with somebody else and the four of us went. I went with an older couple, and we docked at Southampton coming back, and there was this guy waving to me and I was getting the suitcases off and looking to see if I had two bob cause you had to give everybody two bob to carry your suitcases. He lowered me suitcases on this trolley and Barbara said: 'I think he's waving to you.' I said: 'No, no bugger knows me on a bloody cruise.'
I said: 'The only guy who got to know me, I was cheating at deck tennis. I was playing him every day, deck tennis and he said I was overstepping the mark. Anyway, it was Alan Brown on the quayside waving. I went down, he said he was going to sign me for Sunderland. I said I knew nowt about it and I didn't. He said he was going to sign me and that was it.
I thought about it all the way home in the car, in me pal's car. I thought I'd kicked up enough stink at Middlesbrough wanting to get away, I wanted to go in the first division, which I did. Sunderland were going into the first division and I went and signed for them, simple as that.
I enjoyed it there very much. People at Sunderland think I am a Sunderland man, which I wasn't. I'm a Yorkshireman, a Middlesbrough lad, but I had a very, very happy time at Sunderland. They all took to me straight away.
Me two sons were born in Sunderland, my daughter was born in west Hartlepool, so they regard themselves as Northerners, and I was just happy at Sunderland - simple as that. And it showed. It actually came when I had finished playing through injury. They

gave me a testimonial and I got 31,000 there for me testimonial. Now that wasn't bad.

There wasn't five clubs in the country that could get 31,000 for a league match, never mind a testimonial.

BERNIE

Goals continued at Roker Park and you got 53 to your credit. Then you suffered a serious knee injury which ended your career. What was the injury?

CLOUGHIE

I hit a goalkeeper. It was an icy day. One of your lot was in charge, Kevin Howley, and I used to know Kevin very well. We were walking round the pitch, and he asked me what I thought. I said well it was Boxing Day and the bloody crowd was in at 2.30pm I told him he had to put it on, so I influenced him really. So we put it on it was an icy pitch and I got a ball played through from a lad called Jimmy McNab. He couldn't play football to save his life, and I chased it and I wasn't looking at the goalkeeper and I always used to keep my eye on him. And he came and hit me halfway on me knees. I went over him and bust me cruciate ligament and me medial ligament and a cartilage. Now they can do cruciate ligaments, but in my day you couldn't do them and me bloody knee was wobbling about and never became stable. Now they drill the bone and put a knot at the other end, but they couldn't do it then and I finished playing on the Boxing Day. Simple as that.

BERNIE

So how did you cope. You were only 27?

CLOUGHIE

Yeah, well, Mr Brown the surgeon, he set me left leg in plaster from the ankle up to the top. And he set it bent so the medial ligament could heal quickly. Me leg was like that, bent, and I always had big quadriceps and everything so I spent another three months getting me legs straight. I was training on me own, which is a killer training on your own when you're injured. I was going back mornings and afternoons. Brownlee was a right taskmaster. I used to go into the ground at five to 10 in the morning and he'd be standing in his office looking out the window. And he used to come down at 10am, and he used to say: 'I'm waiting on the day I catch you coming in gone 10.' And I always used to get in at five to ten by the time I'd got down the bloody stairs. I'd be saying: 'What time are we going training'

BERNIE

How did you cope with the injury?

CLOUGHIE

When I got injured at Sunderland, George Hardwick was manager and he pulled me in. There was no barrier on wages and I was on £40 a week when I went to Sunderland, which was a fortune. I got injured and I was in plaster and Hardwick called me in. He said: 'If you think you're going to hang around here for a year injured earning £40 a week, you've got another thing coming. He said: "You're in charge of the A team for tomorrow' and this started me off. That's where I met Colin Todd, playing for the A team for Sunderland. Eventually Rolls Royce went bankrupt in Derby, and the whole town went bloody bankrupt, you know it was like the ICI closing down in Middlesbrough. They cleared the building societies out of the money and there was big long queues, everybody was out (of work) and I went back to Sunderland and signed Toddy for £175,000, which was an absolute million.

I came back and the chairman nearly fainted. I said: 'I've done some good business today.' He said: 'What have you done' and I said: 'I've signed a lad called Colin Todd.' He said: 'Oh yes, and who does he play for Brian?

I said: 'He's playing for Derby tomorrow.' He asked me what he cost and I told him. He never spoke to me for a year.

BERNIE

You started your managerial career at Hartlepool, along with ex-Boro goalkeeper Peter Taylor as your No 2. Was that a good place to learn your managerial role?

CLOUGHIE

Well, it was the only job I got offered. I took the job the night I got me testimonial. I took over Hartlepool that night as well. But what broke my heart was, you had a manager called Raich Carter, who once again was an idol in football in general. Raich had played for England, I think he played for Derby, and he played for several clubs anyway. But he was in the Wilf Mannion bracket Raich Carter was and Raich was in charge. The journalists used to go down, as I've already said, on Tuesday and I got a lift down with one of them and went in to see Raich. I said: 'I'm finishing, I've been in charge of the Sunderland youth side for the last six months or whatever, any chance of me coming and starting at Middlesbrough in charge of the youths?' He said: 'Oh, I will ask them.' And he went to a board meeting, I went back the following week and he said: 'No, they won't have you back'. I didn't quite believe him at the time, because I hadn't upset the board of directors or anything. I never saw them from one month to another.

But Raich turned me down for my first job in football, and it set me back of course. I thought, like all footballers, you take your boots off one minute and you become a manager the next. I wanted to be a manager and I knew I wanted to be a manager when I was 25. But Raich turned me down. I could have been sitting where you're sitting now, working for Middlesbrough, if he'd have taken me on. You will never know.

BERNIE

Leaving Hartlepool you steered second division Derby County to promotion, then the first division title in 1972. Was that purely down to your managerial skills, or having quality players, or a mixture?

CLOUGHIE

Well, we signed the players. One of the first players I signed was Roy McFarland from Tranmere. Then I signed Archie Gemmill from Preston, then I got John Robson, he came from Birtley in between Sunderland and Newcastle. We got a Kevin Hector, who came from Bradford, we had a nucleus of a side there and I signed John O'Hare and Colin Todd from Sunderland and Dave Mackay from Tottenham. He was the best one because he was 32 and I was managing a side 21-plus and I was only 30. Dave Mackay was older than me and he was still playing.

BERNIE

You moved to Nottingham Forest, where you won the first division title in 1978, and won the European cup twice in the 1978 and 1979 seasons. How did you do it? You weren't exactly loaded with cash?

CLOUGHIE

Well, we got all the players. I signed Kenny Burns, one of the best signings ever. I was judging a sweet pea show in Nottingham and told him I would meet him at the garden centre where it was being judged. He was coming from Birmingham. He turned up in a car that if the coppers had seen him in they would have arrested him just looking at it. He had no tax disc, one side was all bashed in. I said: 'How about insurance?' He said: 'What's that?' I said: 'Get to the bloody ground, get out of my sight. I will sign you at the ground.' And players used to place an awful lot of trust in me. They used to sign blank forms and I'd say when all the staff come in on Monday I'll fill it all in. And I told them not to worry, that they would get exactly what I promised. And they always signed blank forms, did it for years. I was proud of it actually. So we go to the ground, sign these forms. So I said to Burnsy: 'Right, I'm going back home, it's my bloody day off.' He said: 'Well, give us a couple of pounds of those peas. I'll take them home and give them to the wife and we will have them for lunch tomorrow.' I said: 'They're bloody sweet peas, not the ones you eat!' So that's how we signed Kenny Burns. He was a smashing lad and he comes to see me now. He lives in Derby actually, and he was a good player - what a good player he was. He gave me as much as any body gave me. Bloody hell, he frightened everyone as well. He frightened the Spanish to such an extent. I played against Barcelona in a European cup, not the European Cup we have mentioned, another competition - their champions versus us and beat Barcelona in it. They went out to sort him out in Spain and I was shouting at him to kick the ball, the normal words. There was four going at him and he was whacking it and whacking it and he turned round when he cleared and said to the Spanish - he couldn't speak English never mind Spanish Burnsy couldn't. He said 'You're the next if you come anywhere near me'. And they soon got the message and they scarpered from him.

And he used to give Shilton some stick. He'd say to Shilton: 'You're the best goalkeeper, they tell me you get more money than anybody else at this club. 'Do you know why you're the best goalkeeper?' And Shilton was very quiet in the dressing room and just said 'no'. Kenny was the opposite. Kenny used to give me stick, never mind owt else, and he used to say: 'You're the best goalkeeper because they never get to you.'

'I take all the bloody flak for you, me and Lloydy (Larry Lloyd).' There was Burnsy and Lloydy and if they ever got past the two of them without getting kicked, Shilton used to come out and spread his bloody self and you couldn't see the goal. So they used to miss the bloody target, by about a yard. Burnsy used to say: 'I take all your flak. As a matter of fact, I should get half your wages!'

BERNIE

Trophies followed in the 80s but you were relegated in 1993. Why did you retire after relegation?

CLOUGHIE

Well, I didn't feel as if I had enough time in the game, but I certainly was considering retiring 18 months before I did. I know that it sounds blasé now, but I'd been in management fairly young, you know. I didn't play until I was 25 and then had a quick entry into management. I went into management when I was 30, 31-ish, and I was thrown in at the deep end.

Straight away I was winning first division championships within years of coming to Derby, two or three years. It's ironic actually, because the first two championships, I won one at Derby and I was in the Scilly Isles.

Harold Wilson had told me about the Scilly Isles - I'm a big socialist actually. A bloke at a college once said to me: 'How come you are such a big socialist, driving a Mercedes and

32

smoking a cigar?' Because I went on to my Mercedes and I started smoking when I was about 26.

I said: 'The difference between you, a Tory, and me is I don't mind everybody having a bloody Mercedes and a big cigar. 'You bloody lot who were born with it don't want anybody else to have it!'

Rich people, don't you know, hate other people getting bloody rich and of course I was in my Mercedes with my big cigar. But I was in the Scilly Isles - Harold Wilson said to me that the Scilly Isles would suit me with the kids.

So when I won it with Derby I was in the Silly Isles. Leeds had got done at Wolves, then when I won it at Forest and I was on an aeroplane and there was a match being played and it had to be confirmed. I'd already won it before we left and the pilot was getting the scores and then he sent the girl along to tell me that we couldn't get a reception and that I'd have to wait until we got back to the airport. So I found out we had won the second division and first division when I was in Spain.

I think a few sangrias were involved that week. I never saw the lads when we went away. One famous manager, I won't tell you his name because I thought he was a bit of an amateur, he said: 'What's this business about you not training when you go away?' I said: 'Well, we don't, we don't do a lot.'

He said: 'Well don't you think training is essential?' I said: 'Absolutely. We train five weeks before the season starts, then we play Saturday, Wednesday, Saturday in European cups.' I said: 'And come Christmas we are knackered, and come January and February I can tell the players that's been injured.'

He said: 'How can you tell that?' I said: 'Well, you can walk in the dressing room and the players that have played right up until February are white-faced and the ones that have been injured, you'd think they had just come off a bloody cruise.' They are full of it and never kicked a ball all season. I said: 'We use European matches for a break from the domestic first division', which was hard for us. And it was hard for us every week. Hell, we only had bloody 14 players and we used to go abroad and Burnsy used to say: 'We aren't taking any training gear are we gaffer?' I would tell them just to take a pair of plimsolls and some shorts and we just used to hang around the pool and soak up the sun and then we would go for a walk before our meal and that was our training for four days. When we won the second European Cup I took them all to Spain to Cala Millor for five days and then we flew straight to the European Cup and we never trained one day.

All we wanted was a rest. Come May you're on your knees. I was on my knees and I was only the manager.

BERNIE

Do you think the influx of foreigners is killing the national game?

CLOUGHIE

It's not helped, because we have now become saturated.
I advocated foreigners to our football early on in my managerial career. Before I thought they had something to offer. They had this typically different game with skills. We had our tackling and all that and if I could have merged the two I would have got the best team ever. I said to let a few foreigners come in and we will teach them how to tackle, and how to live and play in the conditions that we have to play football in. Because if there is a shower in Spain they put the match off and things like that. We used to play in bloody snow! But it's gone overboard now, I was with Jim Smith, who was the manager of Derby County and he was on to me again and he said: 'When are you going to start coming to the matches regularly?'
I said: 'The second me foreign language course is finished - I can't pronounce one bloody name of any of your players, there is nine bloody foreigners.' He said: 'I know what you mean.' I

said: 'If I can't pronounce one name, you cant pronounce any because you're worse than me!'

He had nine in the side - nine foreigners. And they were from Czechoslovakia, Romania, Spain, France and all over the bloody place. Sky television have been trying to get me back to work for two years now. And I keep saying to everybody who's trying to get me to work and I don't mean this rudely, that I don't regard this as work with you because I'm one of you. But when you've got to go on television and down to London and all that, that work takes all bloody day to get to London and all day to get back, and I work there three to four hours. So I stopped doing everything and they have been pushing me to go back on television and do commentary, and I saw Ron Atkinson doing the Man Utd commentary one night. I've been to Graz, because we beat them in the European cup I think Graz one year. But it's a different ball game now - all bloody foreigners. And as I say, the nearest I could come to pronouncing a foreign name is spaghetti, and I like spaghetti. But some of the foreigners I don't like and your lot always get a mention.

Middlesbrough always get a mention. When I'm talking I say they go to Middlesbrough and they sign on the dotted line and they get their £20,000 left in a bank somewhere and they get well paid from Middlesbrough.

There wives go out one morning and it's pouring down and then she goes out the next morning and it's snowing and she says she can't live in this climate, I've got to go home. And he has now buggered off cause of the climate.

BERNIE

Well, Ravanelli, Juninho and Emerson all went and Juninho has returned now.

CLOUGHIE

Yes, and we had a lot of time for him. We think you got rid of the wrong one, because now he's come back we are delighted. Is he a good player?

BERNIE

Oh, he's a quality player, no doubting that. The game against Chesterfield was going to be between 8-10,000. With his name on the team sheet, 25,000 turned up.

CLOUGHIE
Brilliant, brilliant. My sister would have been there shouting for him.

BERNIE

Is that the one who stopped me in the bus station and said: 'Bernie you were a good player, but not as good as my brother!'

CLOUGHIE

It's got to be her. I've only got two sisters and she's the oldest sister.
It's got to be her. She used to come to Nottingham Forest with her country cousin every match. My PR girl used to come to me and say: 'Your sister's here with her country cousin.' I said: 'Well, I don't want to see them. Tell them I'm in the bath, anything. And they all used to have a fag. Coming from Middlesbrough they all had a bloody fag like, you know? Because everybody had nowt else to do up there apart from smoke or go for a pint. They would be sitting there saying Forest weren't playing very well and we were beating Arsenal, somebody like that. You'd be in the second division as you were

when I was at Forest and then we would take on Liverpool and beat Liverpool and then we would take on all the top clubs and they used to be sitting there in the directors' box saying we weren't as good as Boro. I'd say: 'Bloody Boro. You're bottom half of the second division!' And I used to get annoyed with them. They enjoyed their days out, but of course I didn't mind them coming down, even though they were family and fantastic Boro supporters and season ticket holders, simple as that. And they tell me I've never been to tour the new stadium.

They tell me its beautiful. The strides you have made since I was a player. We used to train at a place called Hutton Road - well, I used to train there and it was a trek to get from Ayresome Park to Hutton Road. In fact, I used to ask occasionally if I could go straight to Hutton Road, because I was nearer Hutton Road than I was Ayresome Park.

But there was no chance. When you got in you might have a pair of boots to clean. (Lindy) Delapenha used to throw his boots at me and tell me to get them clean. I became very friendly with Rolando Ugolini because he was a character. A smashing fella. He made a special effort to come and see me in Scotland last time I was there and we were playing. He got on the coach and I said: 'Hey, I'm the bloody manager of this side' like, you know?

BERNIE

Did he give you a tip?

CLOUGHIE

No tip. Oh, they gave me one tip. Keep off the M1 when it's foggy. They gave me that one year. It's the best bloody tip I got!

BERNIE
Last question Brian. Do you still have a soft spot for Middlesbrough?

CLOUGHIE

I do, because my family's there, born and bred there.
You can never lose that, where you are born and bred.
I phoned a guy up when he was 90-odd at Middlesbrough, a
school teacher called Grant and he signed me for
Middlesbrough. George Camsell was in charge. Grant was just
an amateur when I was playing for Middlesbrough's third team,
or kids, as it was in those days. But Grant got my signature and
our Doreen, busy bollocks, rang and told me Mr Grants was
going to be 90-odd this one week. I phoned him up and he
couldn't believe. He said he couldn't believe it was me and I
told him I hadn't been up for years so I hadn't seen him. He told
me that I sounded just the same on the telephone and I told him I
hadn't changed. I'm still Middlesbrough through and through. A
born and bred Yorkshireman and proud of it. I wished I was
back playing for Middlesbrough.

HONOURS

BRIAN HOWARD CLOUGH

PLAYING CAREER HISTORY

1955-1961   Middlesbrough
1961-1964   Sunderland
1957-1958   England U23
1957   England B
1959   England

MANAGERIAL CAREER HISTORY

1965-1967   Hartlepool United
1967-1973   Derby County
1973-1974   Brighton and Hove Albion
1974   Leeds
1975-1993   Nottingham Forest

MANAGERIAL HONOURS (winners)

Nottingham Forest
1976-1977   Division 2 Promotion
1977-1978   League Champions
1977-1978   League Cup
1978-1979   European Cup
1978-1979   League Cup
1979-1980   European Cup
1979-1980   European Super Cup
1988-1989 League Cup
1988-1989 Simod Cup
1989-1990 League Cup
1991-1992 Zenith Data Cup
CAPS 2 Full caps for England
BRIAN CLOUGH OBE,MA

The League Trophy

Brian Clough and Bill Shankly leading their teams out.

"So I like to think that my criticism was justified and my words hit the target and contributed to the building of Rockliffe Park."

Referring to previous training grounds.

FABRIZIO RAVANELLI
MIDDLESBROUGH

Fabrizio Ravanelli born 11th December,1968, in Perugia Italy.
He signed from Juventus in July 1996, for a fee of seven
million, he settled into life on Teesside instantly, scoring a
hatrick in his premier league debut against Liverpool, his
nickname was the white feather and his goal celebration and
trademark was the best I have witnessed, pulling his shirt over
his head after every goal, exposing his well toned torso.
After scoring thirty one goals in 1996- 97 season, he departed
and joined Olympique Marseille.

I travelled to Rome to meet the white feather.

I met up with him in the training ground. When I witnessed the
facilities, I could understand his criticism of Boro. I awaited his
arrival, Rav pulled up in his Ferrari, jumped out casually.
He was smartly dressed, eyes camouflaged with a pair of
designer glasses, we shook hands and carried on with the
interview.

Rav for me was a colourful character, confident, outspoken and
at times outrageous, his English was limited therefore I needed a
translator, Sergio travelled with us from Middlesbrough in fact
he studied in Middlesbrough and was a relation of Ravs, small
world don't you think.

BERNIE

You had to wait until you were 24 to make your Serie A debut.
Why did it take you so long to make a first team breakthrough?

RAVANELLI

Well, because in those days football was different at the end of
the 1980s and the beginning of the 1990s. It was difficult for
young football players to play in Serie A. At the age of 20 there

were few young players around. Now it has all changed. Now young players are given a chance quite easily
by clubs.

BERNIE

You went to Juventus in 1992. Would you class that as a dream move?

RAVANELLI

Yes, it was a dream at that time.
Nowadays and in the history of football Juventus have always been one of the greatest clubs in Italy and in the world.I used to support Juventus so it was a fantastic, dream move. I remember my first day there. I was sweating and shaking and very, very nervous playing alongside the likes of Gianluca
Vialli, Roberto Baggio and David Platt - it was fantastic. I settled in gradually and then established myself as a first team player. The time at Juventus was very satisfactory for me.

BERNIE

You scored in the European Cup Final. Was that the highlight of your club career?

RAVANELLI

Talking about that at this very moment sends shivers down my spine.
It had always been a dream to score in the Champions League Final.
As we were progressing through the rounds, having already scored five goals in that competition, I was thinking all the time about playing and maybe scoring in the final. I knew that we

would play the final in Rome, in the Olympic Stadium, with a fantastic atmosphere similar to Wembley. Therefore that goal stands out as one of the greatest moments in my career and I hope to have the chance one day to do it again. I am in great shape now and hope to keep playing like I am at present and hopefully win trophies with Lazio like I did with Juventus.

BERNIE

Where did the nickname the White Feather come from, or is it obvious?

RAVANELLI

Because of my hair, but also because when Roberto Bettega, one of my idols, used to play for Juventus he also had grey hair and this nickname. They associated my image with Bettega, and gave me the nickname White Feather.

BERNIE

You left Juventus and joined Boro for a fee of £7 million. Why did you come to Teesside, was it money or ambition?

RAVANELLI

No, it wasn't for money even though it is something important for a
football player. It was a fancy of mine. I had always been captain at Juventus. I had played many important games, like for instance in the Bernabeu Stadium in front of 120,000 spectators. I was a very important player, a protagonist. One day, the Juventus and Fiat chairman rang me up saying I would be the future of Juventus - the new captain. I was so happy.

Then in the summer while I was on holiday I was reading in the papers that I was about to sign for Middlesbrough. Juventus wouldn't tell me anything, they had already agreed everything without even informing me. I was very disappointed. Then when the Boro representative came to talk to me in Milan I totally believed everything Bryan Robson, who I hold in high esteem, said to me. My only mistake was not seeing the training facilities and the training methods at Boro before signing. They told me that Boro would be a success story, a new force in the English Premiership and in Europe, like Parma in Italy. But things worked out differently to how they were represented to me.

BERNIE

You scored a hat-trick against Liverpool on your Middlesbrough debut. Is that your best-ever debut?

RAVANELLI

I also scored a hat-trick on my debut for Reggiana against Verona. It wasn't the first time I'd scored a hat-trick on my debut. But I think to score against Liverpool was surely the most important. My very first game in England in a different league and country. Yes, a sensational debut.

BERNIE

You forged a great partnership with Juninho. How good was Juninho?

RAVANELLI

He is a fantastic player. I don't know why he didn't have success in Spain because I rate Juninho as one of the best footballers in the world. It was very important for me to play alongside him. Many of the goals I scored were thanks to Juninho. He is a wonderful player and a very good person. I think in order to exploit his skills to the maximum, you have to play him in a position that suits him.

BERNIE

Some people said that Juninho and Emerson were the only two players on the same wavelength as you. Would you agree?

RAVANELLI

Well, there were many important players in that squad, not only me Juninho and Emerson. We were obviously the most well known. I was a bit disappointed when Nick Barmby was sold, he was a very talented footballer who played for the team, who could have provided me with loads of assists and great goals. There were other important players who worked hard like Robbie Mustoe - maybe he had something more - but all the other players were important as well. In my opinion, if we had a player like Barmby in the squad perhaps with Juninho and myself, without being disrespectful to other players, we could have been the best attack in the league. We played together the three of us in some very good matches against Everton and Liverpool for example. At the beginning of the season we were doing very well in the league and Barmby was playing. We were very well positioned in the league and it was a pleasant surprise for everybody. Barmby was scoring goals, I was scoring goals, Juninho was scoring goals, we were three complementary players and I don't know why he was sold.

BERNIE

I must ask you about your relationship with Mikkel Beck. You used to point your finger at him during games.

RAVANELLI

I was always trying to liven him up a bit. I was trying to help him understand - also in training - the way we were trying to play together. My gestures were not intended to blame him, he was a bit of a strange lad, very reserved. You just could not manage to understand what he was thinking. He had some good footballing skills, but he did not have a great personality on the pitch. I have absolutely nothing against him, maybe if he had tried to understand me in a different way, for all the things I used to say to him were intended for his own good.
When playing he would only think about scoring a goal and that was not necessarily a good thing. Of course it is an important thing for an attacking player to score, especially for self confidence. But a centre forward must primarily think about what is good for the team. If I have the opportunity to pass the ball to a team mate for him to score, then I do it, I pass the ball to him not being selfish. And if I'm not mistaken many of the goals he scored were from my assists so
it is clear that I was trying to help him.

BERNIE

Who were you closest to at Boro?

RAVANELLI

One player I got on very well with was Gianluca Festa. He is an Italian, like me. I also got on very well with Juninho.

49

I had no particular problems with Steve Vickers, Robbie
Mustoe, I had no problems whatsoever with most of the players.
There were some
players who tried to make things up about me. I remember one
time
coming back from a match playing in Naples in Italy for the
national team. It was a very important qualifying match for the
World Cup against Poland.
I had to come back to Middlesbrough the day after the match.
The match was delayed and ended up late at night. From Naples
there were no flights available to come back until the next day.
I want to share this episode with you, which will make people
realise that jealousy was present in the dressing room. One
player - whose name I'm not going to tell, but if he was
reading this interview would
recognise himself - said on the eve of the match against Aston
Villa, a very important game, that I did not behave like a
professional for not returning straight back to Middlesbrough.
He said that in the papers and I got very angry. We won that
match and I scored three goals and took the
responsibility to kick a penalty in injury time, a huge
responsibility.
Maybe someone was jealous and wanted to cover for their own
mistakes by putting the blame on me.

BERNIE

Where did your goalscoring celebration come from, pulling your
shirt over your head? And would you do it if you had a big
belly?

RAVANELLI

No, if I had a beer belly, I would not. I was playing in a match with Juventus against Napoli and the manager told me to calm down at half-time. The whole team was very nervous, the score was 0-0 and it looked like we couldn't score. Then he said to me that only some magic from a top class player would resolve the match. With five minutes remaining I scored a great goal, so his prediction was right. By instinct I lifted my shirt up and since then I've kept on doing it every time I score a goal.

BERNIE

You went on record as saying Middlesbrough's training facilities and methods were poor. What exactly did you mean?

RAVANELLI

Every criticism that came from me was directed at trying to improve things, a constructive criticism. I remember when I arrived in Middlesbrough from Juventus, such a big club with top training and medical facilities.
I had to drive to the Riverside Stadium, get changed, drive in my car to Tollesby and train in a meadow surrounded by houses and people walking their dogs and asking for autographs. That was unacceptable. You can't fully concentrate in a situation like that. All I wanted was people to understand that if you want to be successful you need to have top training and medical facilities. Recently I saw a programme on Italian TV showing the new wonderful facilities at Rockliffe Park. So I like to think that my criticism was justified and my words hit the target and contributed to the building of Rockliffe Park.

BERNIE

Do you regret your comments about pollution on Teesside?

RAVANELLI

I never said such things. I only said that the town was different from say London or Rome. I was happily settled and felt at ease on Teesside as I was living in a beautiful countryside village - Hutton Rudby - next door to Gordon McQueen. I was happy. Middlesbrough is an industrial town and surely I won't tell a lie about the fact that there might be a little bit of pollution. But in saying this I don't want to offend anyone. Every town has its own history and culture which you have to respect. I was very happy in Middlesbrough and I want to stress it now that I have a microphone in front of me, so that no body can go and change or twist my words. Every time I am interviewed my words are different. Now either I am insane - which I am not - or there are individuals around who enjoy twisting my words. The interpreter who I had at Middlesbrough is also here and he can testify that for instance one time we did an interview which turned out to be completely twisted and misinterpreted in the papers. Allegedly I had claimed that English players were all drunks. It was just a load of rubbish. I don't know, maybe people in the English press didn't like me and speculated by misquoting me as soon as they had the chance.

BERNIE

People respect you as a player and top goalscorer, but also consider you arrogant and ignorant, a bit of a big head. Is that a fair assessment?

RAVANELLI

Maybe that is what people think of me in England but certainly
in Italy and France people don't think I am like that at all.
I have never had a problem with the Italian or French press, only
in England I had a problem and I don't know the reason why.
I want to say it once again - I was happy in England at Boro.
Yes, I had some differences which people know the reasons
about, so I won't waste time explaining them. The only big
regret I have is that I left on not very good terms with the fans.
Because I love the people of Teesside, I love Boro supporters,
and I would love one day to return to Middlesbrough and repay
the debt that I've got with the fans. Because in spite of the 31
goals that I scored I was bitterly sorry that we were relegated.

BERNIE

You were part of the team which was beaten in two cup finals
and got relegated. What went wrong?

RAVANELLI

Let's say it as it is. I don't mean any offence or disrespect, but
the reason we lost the League Cup lies entirely with Bryan
Robson. He's a good person, but when your team are winning a
cup final in the 119th minute with a chance of making history
for Middlesbrough Football Club, you have to use your
substitutes. We had three substitutions to make. Emerson was
limping, he should have taken him off. He didn't and we didn't
win. He didn't know what he was doing at the end of the match.
It was not important which player had to come off, we had the
possibility to make three changes and we didn't make one.
One change every 20 seconds, three changes. The referee would
have blown the whistle, the game was over.

BERNIE

You scored 31 goals in total. Was that more than you anticipated?

RAVANELLI

Yes, more than I expected. I didn't expect to get 31 goals with a team that eventually got relegated. I was at the peak of my career, on very fine form, and I also had a player alongside me like Juninho who helped me score goals.

BERNIE

Why did you leave Middlesbrough and did you leave on good terms?

RAVANELLI

I left because I wanted to play in the World Cup and by playing in the First Division there was no chance for me. I left by telling the chairman and the manager that I wanted to remain a Boro player by going on loan for a year and coming back to Middlesbrough after that. They didn't want to, never mind.

BERNIE

Would you like to return to England one day as a player or manager?

RAVANELLI

Yes, I would like to do both, maybe at Middlesbrough with Bryan Robson.

HONOURS.

FABRIZIO RAVANELLI.

PLAYING CAREER HISTORY

1986-1989   Perugia
1989   Avellino
1989-1990   Casertana
1990-1991   Avellino
1991-1992   Reggiana
1992-1996   Juventus
1996-1998   Middlesbrough
1998-2000   Marseille
2000-2001   SS Lazio
2001-2003   Derby County
2003   Dundee FC
2004-2005   Perugia

PLAYING HONOURS (winners)

Juventus
1996 Champions League
1993 UEFA Cup
1995 Italian SuperCup
1995 Serie A Champions
1995 Italian Cup

SS Lazio
2000 Serie A Champions
2000 Italian Cup

CAPS 22 Full caps for Italy

Ravanelli, typical goal celebration.

Rav playing for Middlesbrough.

"I honestly believe when a manager signs his own players he almost wants them to do better than the players who were already in the squad, so he can justify the transfer fee."

Referring to players bought by the club

BERNIE SLAVEN
MIDDLESBROUGH

I was born 13th november1960, in Paisley Scotland. After floating about the Scottish lower divisions, I joined Middlesbrough for a fee of twenty five thousand back in 1984/85.I got off to a good start in my home debut against Bradford in a 1-1 draw.Throughout my time at Middlesbrough the team faced relegation,liquidation and promotion.
After I retired I have been heavily involved with media work.

For this interview I asked a couple of North East media colleagues to write me some questions.

What was it like growing up in Glasgow?

BERNIE

I had a brilliant upbringing. I was brought up on a council estate called Castlemilk. My dad worked for the Co-Op delivering and my ma was a tailoress by trade. My dad introduced me to football at a tender age and took me on a regular basis to see Celtic. He would perch me on the wall at the front of the Rangers End - the away end at Parkhead - with a packet of sweets, tell me not to move and say he would see me at the end of the game after he stood with his mates on the terrace. Celtic was so packed in those days that if you needed a pee you had to do it in your trousers. Dad took me to see the European Cup semi-final against Leeds at Hampden Park in 1969/70, when a record 136,505 crowd turned up. Celtic won 2-1 on the night for a 3-1 aggregate score and dad was as good as his word - he took me to the San Siro for the final, where Celtic lost to Feyenoord. It was an unforgettable experience. Living on the estate wasn't all good memories. Some of my mates were glue sniffing, taking drugs. In fact, one of my mates died young due to hepatitis through using a dirty needle. I loved my dad, but I was also frightened of him. He would give me a time when I had to be in and if I was late, he would belt my arse.

Literally take the belt off his trousers, bend me over and lash me. Could you imagine doing that in this day and age? You can't hit your kid with a feather now! I'm sure I would have ended up on drugs and drink and gone off the rails if it wasn't for my dad. He kept me on the straight and narrow. Looking back at my time on that rough council estate and my upbringing, it has made me mentally tough, appreciate things and taught me never to get too big for my boots. I might have lived in Teesside for the last 25 years, but I'm still the boy from that council estate. My pockets may have changed, but my mentality hasn't. Theres a saying that I picked up in Glasgow and I have carried it with me for years: "I'm better than no one and no one is better than me." I despise big time Charlies.

How did you get into football and how rapidly did you progress up the ladder?

BERNIE

I got into football at an early age, but my progression was gradual. I started off playing for my primary school team, St Dominic's. Believe it or not, I played left-back. When I moved to St Margaret Mary's secondary school I played at left half, just tucked inside the winger. I also played at amateur level for a team called Eastercraigs. They were on a par with Celtic Boys' Club. The manager was a guy called Bill Livingston.
He liked a cigarette and during the games he would rip the cigarette box apart and scribble notes on the back of it! Bill actually predicted that two players from that team would turn professional. Graeme Sharp joined Dumbarton and went on to Everton fame and I was advised to go to the Northern League to toughen up. I did, playing for Rutherglen and Glencairn, before turning professional with Greenock Morton. My time in the Northern League certainly toughened me up. Back then you were allowed to tackle from behind and I was forever getting

walloped. To combat that I used to wear shin pads at the back as well as the front! That experience certainly put me in good stead for what lay ahead in the professional game.

Who were the most important people in your football development?

BERNIE

Mr Kelly at primary school taught me the basics. I have already mentioned Bill Livingston, Eastercraig's manager.
He instilled a bit of discipline in me, polished up my fitness and encouraged me to get forward. I remember Bill pulled me aside one day and said I had a great left foot and could pick a lock with it. Then on another occasion, he said I was the only midfielder he knew that scored three and the guy I was marking scores four. I don't think that was complimentary! Last, but not least, my dad. He encouraged me, trained me and believed that one day I would become a professional.
The best advice I got as youngster was from my dad, who taught me how to pass to a team-mate with the inside of my boot. He was forever telling me you don't have to bust the ball, pass it, and that stayed with me throughout my career.

You ended up becoming the top scorer in Scottish football with Albion Rovers but were frozen out of the first team because of a dispute. Talk about a strange situation!

BERNIE

Without a doubt. After scoring 31 goals and finishing Scotland's top goalscorer, I reckoned there would have been a host of clubs wanting my signature. But according to the chairman at the time, a guy called Tom Fagan, who had similar traits to the Oliver Twist character, there was no interest whatsoever. At the end of that season I picked up the club's Player Of The Year and top scorer award and the Second Division Player Of The Year award. But there was still no sign of a move. I was offered a new contract by Albion Rovers, but it was on the same money. I refused point blank to sign it. Even if it had trebled I wouldn't have signed. After turning down the contract, Albion banned me from training. So I had to train on my own up until I got my move south to Middlesbrough. I could have understood being banned from linking up with my team-mates if I had been fighting or I had broken club rules.

But the only thing that I had broken was the club goal scoring record, and here I was being treated like a leper because I wasn't signing. Incidentally, the contract being offered was £70 a week. What a f*****g joke. The whole situation I found myself in was unbelievable.

How close were you to quitting football and working full-time in your day job as a gardener?

BERNIE

I had promised myself if I didn't get a club I would hang up my boots and I was serious. Surely banging in goals galore for a team who were rated one of the worst in Britain was a greater achievement than scoring goals for the Old Firm? I questioned my own ability at times. What was I lacking? Was it pace, toughness, aerial ability? I knew I had deficiencies and that certain parts of my game needed polishing, but I always believed there was a place in the game for goalscorers. And in my favour I had a good left peg, which was a rarity. Despite my alienation from Albion I continued to train every day as hard as I could, believing that I would get a break and an opportunity to climb the footballing ladder.

Apart from my part-time football I had a part-time job working with the council tidying gardens.

But my ambition and dream was to become a full-time professional footballer.

Boro were the only side who gave you a positive reply to your letters.

BERNIE

As the new season got underway I remained an outcast. Then out of the blue a guy from the Weekly News called Andrew Gold got in touch with me and did a couple of interviews and wrote a couple of articles asking why Scotland's top goalscorer hadn't got a club. Eventually he approached me with an idea - draft a letter up and send it to every First and Second Division club in England and the Premier up in Scotland. I refused. I wasn't begging for a job. I'd scored 31 goals and if I couldn't get there on merit, forget it, I will chuck it. A week later Andrew turned up at my parents' house with a host of stamped addressed envelopes to all the clubs north and south of the border. Inside each was a letter which he asked me to sign. I relented and agreed to sign all 54 letters. He sent them off and all I could do was sit back and hope and pray that I would get some positive replies and get an invite for a trial. Over the next week the letters started to drop through my parents' door. Every one of the clubs who got back in touch refused to invite me for a trial - QPR, Stoke, Sheff Wed, Watford. The list went on.
They all explained that they were full up with strikers and wished me luck in my search for a club. Only one Scottish club replied, that was Hearts. Not even my boyhood heroes Celtic had the decency to reply. That really pissed me off. Middlesbrough didn't reply by letter, they phoned me up. The chief scout Barry Geldart invited me for a trial. Eleven days after sending the letters I was heading for Middlesbrough.

How daunting was it coming to Teesside?

BERNIE

There is no doubting it was daunting coming to Teesside. I remember coming in on the train and seeing the smog and cooling towers and thinking: "What the f*** is this I've come to?" I remember walking into the dressing room with a big, long herring bone coat on, that I bought in a market in Glasgow for a tenner, I think. And my boots were in a plastic bag. I could see a few for the young pros like Colin Cooper and Alan Kernaghan wondering who the hippy was.

After a couple of days' training I travelled to play against Grimsby Town down at Blundell Park in a reserve fixture. We lost 1-0 and I didn't exactly set the heather alight. The following day I caught the train back to Glasgow, even though the club wanted me to stay for a month to take a proper look at me. But I didn't want to gamble or take the chance in case I lost my job with the council. My dad went ballistic and told me it was my last chance. I was 24, f*** the council.

I left Willie Maddren a message on his answering machine saying I wouldn't be back and returned to work. Out of the blue I got another call on the Monday asking me to travel down for one more trial game against Bradford at Ayresome Park. We gubbed Bradford 4-0, I scored two and set up two for Archie Stephens. The following morning I signed a two-year contract with a two-year option which favoured the club. I had trebled my wages with one decent 90-minute performance.

After signing it didn't take me long to establish that the club were struggling, not just on the park but off it as well.

At the end of my first season we were relegated and the club went into liquidation. My whole future was in question once again.

Things were so bad the PFA had to step in and pay our wages. We picked them up from the Town Hall as the gates at Ayresome

Park were locked. Bruce Rioch, the manager, still coached us in places like Stewart Park and Longlands College and we had to wash our own gear. They were dark days but it shaped our characters and the bond in the dressing room was unbelievable. Thankfully the club was saved by a consortium of local businesses. I heard the news first via a bulletin on the news. Unbelievable.

How did you find the transition from Scottish football to English football?

BERNIE

It was tough initially. I remember going for a meal in Middlesbrough after we had returned from my first game at Leeds and I couldn't believe how drained I felt. I remember saying I hoped every game wasn't going to be as difficult as that one. The fitness of the opposing players was great. The pace of the game, the atmosphere. You have to remember I had always been a part-timer and I had trained on my own for a couple of months. If the truth be known, I wanted to return home to my parents at one point.
I was staying in digs with a family and hated it. The team I was in was poor, my social life was nil. I used to stay in bed on a Sunday, read all the newspapers and sleep. It was partly my own fault because I didn't drive. My first season was difficult on and off the park. But after that initial season I came to terms with the game and the area.

You were top scorer for six consecutive seasons, which is some achievement. How proud are you of your Boro record? You wore the No 7 shirt, scored 147 goals and seven hat-tricks.

BERNIE

Obviously im delighted, to arrive on Teesside as an unknown and end up in the company of Middlesbrough greats, like Fenton, Camsell, Clough and Hickton is no mean feat.I am proud of my Boro record and personally think its a greater achievement banging in goals for a time that was full of home grown talent as apposed to overseas millionaires.

Through an Irish grandfather, you ended up playing international football for the Republic of Ireland and went to the 1990 World Cup in Italy. What was that whole experience like and what was it like playing under Jack Charlton?

BERNIE

I was 29 when I got the opportunity to gain a cap. I honestly thought my opportunity had gone.
The Middlesbrough fans had been chanting 'Bernie for Scotland' but nothing seemed to be happening.
I'd scored 18 goals in the top flight and was third in the division behind John Aldridge and Alan Smith.
Scotland had assured me I would get a B cap at least.
A week later I bumped into Jack Charlton, who told me he would give me a full cap against Wales. He was aware of my Irish connections, so I ended up having a choice.
Scotland had never done anything for me as an individual - I had to come to England to ply my trade.
I was a Celtic fan, Ireland wore green and white and had a better squad with guys like Paul McGrath, Ronnie Whelan and Ray Houghton, so I chose the Republic.
Jack told me that if I did well for Ireland I would go to the World Cup and he was as good as his word.

My debut came against Wales in a 1-0 victory and before I knew
it I was part of the World Cup squad that travelled to Italy.
Big Jack was a real character. He could be a manager one
minute and you listened to him, then he would be your mate the
next minute and he was having a Guinness with you.
Not a lot of managers can do that.

**What were your thoughts on Bruce Rioch's sacking in
February 1990. Boro had qualified for the ZDS Final at
Wembley but were in relegation danger and just lost at home
to Port Vale.**

BERNIE

I was absolutely gutted about Bruce's departure. After all, he
had led us to the Twin Towers for the first time in the club's
history, and that was no mean feat. Admittedly we were
struggling in the league. We were fourth bottom of the
Second Division. Players weren't responding in the same way to
Bruce. The lads were growing up and some were starting to
rebel. I remember being stitched up in a national newspaper
article saying that I never got on with Bruce and I was glad to
see the back of him not long after he had been sacked and I was
boiling. If I had said it - and I've said it about other players and
managers over the years - I would have stuck by it. But I never
uttered those words.
I saw Bruce outside Ayresome Park a couple of days after he had
been sacked and thought he was liable to chin me.
He told me I'd had a lot to say for myself and I was genuinely
annoyed and upset that he believed I would have a go at him
behind his back.
Any problems I had with Bruce I would always tell him to his
face. Maybe that's why he was so annoyed. He knew my
makeup - I would stab you in the heart, not the back.

I got Bruce's phone number from the club secretary and rang him to explain what had happened.

He asked me for the reporter's name and thanked me for phoning. The most important thing for me was he believed what I had told him regarding the article.

Not long after the call, I received a letter from Bruce thanking me for my efforts during his time with the club.

Amazingly, he started the letter with 'Dear Mr Slaven' instead of 'Bernie'. I suppose that was Bruce, you could never read him. One day he would say 'good morning' to you and the next he would blank you. He was unpredictable, but that's what I liked about Sir Bruce.

Lennie Lawrence then came in and pretty much alienated you from his opening speech to the players before his first training session. Describe your relationship with Lennie, because he didn't play you much.

BERNIE

Lennie arrived to take over from Colin Todd in July 1991. I took an instant dislike to him after his initial team meeting.

He said he was looking for new idols. I don't know what the other experienced players like Mogga and Ripley were thinking, but I knew immediately that I was on borrowed time, along with a few others. As the months rolled on, my gut instinct was proved right. Colin Cooper departed for Millwall, Mogga joined Celtic and Mark Proctor, Gary Parkinson and myself were axed for a league game at Brighton. Lennie had signed Paul Wilkinson from Watford, to link up with me supposedly.

I found myself on the bench, with Rippers up the middle. I confronted Lennie on several occasions, like at Bristol City.

I'd been left out of the 14 - rightly or wrongly - for the first time in seven years and Lennie didn't have the courtesy to pull me to one side and tell me to my face.

I told him that his problem was that he was a former school teacher and had never played the game.

The scored ended up 1-1 that night and after that verbal attack we lost respect for each other. We made it into the Premier League that season, so obviously he was doing something right.Despite only giving me 28 starts, I finished up top scorer for the sixth consecutive season with 16 goals.

He must have been absolutely pissed off. That's why I think he played Wilko every game that campaign, hoping he would beat me, and I told him that to his face.

I honestly believe when a manager signs his own players he almost wants them to do better than the players who were already in the squad, so he can justify the transfer fee.

Lennie let me go the following season in the Premier League, and that was despite having only one striker on the books - Wilko.

You ended up moving to Port Vale before Boro had been relegated from the Premier League. How big a wrench was it to leave?

BERNIE

I was gutted, but I had no option. I was being forced out and when you're not wanted there is no point staying.

It's like staying with a woman who doesn't love you. The quicker you get out, the better.

The move to Port Vale wasn't as clear cut as some people made out. I'd talked to Bruce Rioch, who was managing Bolton at the time, and Ossie Ardiles, who was in charge of West Bromwich Albion. I also spoke to my old Boro team-mate Stuart Ripley, who was at Blackburn, and he said their manager Kenny Dalglish was quizzing him about me as Alan Shearer was injured. The papers were also carrying stories saying Brian

Clough was interested in me joining Nottingham Forest, and there was a host of other links.

But the down side to the interest was that they only wanted me until the end of the season.

I was looking for at least a two-year contract and a bit of security.

How did you find it in the Potteries? Didn't one of your teammates chin you on the training ground one day?

BERNIE

Port Vale wasn't a great experience. I stayed in digs with a family for the first three or four months and I was 32 at the time, not a young kid. Later on I rented a place but, if I am being brutally honest, I never really settled, especially off the park.

I enjoyed it on the pitch. We played good football and played at Wembley twice in a week, winning the Autoglass Trophy against Stockport and losing the play-off final against West Brom.

Regarding being chinned, we had a behind closed doors game one day between the first team and the reserves.

A guy called Peter Swan, who in the main was a first team regular, was in the reserves side and I could understand his frustration in playing with the stiffs.

Swanny fouled me for a penalty which I stuck away about 20 minutes into the game and, as I jogged back to the centre circle for the kick-off, Martin Foyle said Swan would do me the next chance he got. He did, in an aerial challenge within a few minutes of the restart. I got up, went right up to him and said: "Because you are 6ft 4in and built like a brick shit house, you think everyone is scared of you. Well, I'm not." I dropped my guard as the manager John Rudge was trying to calm things down, and just at that point Swanny punched me full-on from about two feet away.

Instantly I could see the birds circling above my head, like in the cartoons. I pointed at him and told him he was going to get knee-capped. When we returned to the dressing room he was full of apologies. I told him I could understand his frustration, but if he had wanted to punch someone it should have been the manager! We were pals again after.

You ended up moving back to the North-east and joining Darlington. How hungry were you still at that stage of your career and how serious was the back problem which forced you to retire in 1995?

BERNIE

I had indicated to John Rudge that I was missing Middlesbrough. I still had a house there and returned at every opportunity. He told me to keep it quiet and he would see what he could do. I kept it quiet up until we played Southampton in an FA Cup replay at Vale Park. We won 1-0 and I scored the winner. When I faced the national press afterwards, I couldn't resist the opportunity to say I wanted to return to the North East. My comments appeared in the papers and I was quizzed about them in the manager's office. Fairly soon Rudgie told me that Falkirk, who were odds on to get promotion into the Scottish Premier League, were interested.
I told him point blank I didn't want to return north of the border and that I wanted to go back to the North East, to Darlington or Hartlepool. Don't forget, I was nearly 34. I ended up at Darlington but it wasn't a professional move. It turned into a nightmare. Training every day was taking its toll. I was having spasms in my buttocks and my hamstring wasn't comfortable. Eventually I had a scan which showed two of my discs at the base of my spine had corroded. Taking medical advice, I decided to retire. I still thoroughly enjoy playing and can still play charity games and five-a-side. I can still train, but I'm in bits afterwards. I have a problem with numbing and pins and needles

down my legs. But there are people a lot worse off then me and as long as I can still do a little bit, I'm happy.

You can be a notoriously difficult man to please. What would Bernie Slaven the football fan have made of Bernie Slaven the player?

BERNIE

If I was a football fan having to watch Bernie Slaven play every week, I would have demanded my money back!
No, seriously, it's a great question. I think I would have been infuriated at the number of times he got caught offside.
I would have been frustrated with the number of times he failed when trying to win the ball in the air because he had no bottle.
I would have criticised him for being predominantly left-footed and I would have had a go at his lack of workrate outside the box. On the flip side of the coin, I would have said he possessed a good first touch, could beat a man, cross a good ball, hold the ball up, create and score goals. I think I would look at his price tag as well and question if he was value for money. Looking at his statistics I would argue he has been Middlesbrough's most productive cheap player in the club's history.
That's open to debate, but that would have been my opinion on Bernie Slaven. And I almost forgot - his goal celebration wasn't bad either!

After you career you became a football pundit on the radio. How does commentating on games compare to being out there playing in them?

BERNIE

There's no comparison. When you play football you are in control of your own destiny to a degree.

You burn up energy and get rid of your frustration and of course as a striker you can become a hero or a villain. The adrenaline rush as a professional player is fantastic.

The camaraderie and pranks inside the dressing room are brilliant as well. I have seen Ralgex rubbed inside a player's boxer shorts and when they have put them on after coming out of the shower they have nearly burnt their Davina McCall's off! Socks would get cut up, boots nailed to the floor. Trevor Putney even pissed on me once when I was stretching my groin in the pouring rain in training! Analysing games on the radio is certainly a lot easier than playing it, and

sometimes my comments have been totally misconstrued by the time they got back to the player concerned.

I remember after a Wednesday night cup game at the Riverside I was sat at the back of the stand doing a phone-in and Mark Schwarzer and the goalkeeping coach Paul Barron were going through their warm-down on the pitch.

All of a sudden about half a dozen balls were heading in my direction, although none of Schwarzer's kicks hit me!

I have had ding-dongs with employees of the club because of my strong opinions. Steve McClaren fell out with me.

The way I look at it is I have got two boys who I love more than anything, but when I watch them play football and they are crap I let them know. If I can criticise my sons, why can't I criticise millionaires? Nobody likes criticism. But I'm a fan and an ex-player and my opinions are right down the middle.

I don't say things for effect, I only give my honest opinions. If people agree, great, and if they don't, that's fine.

I commentated on 500 Middlesbrough games and like to think I was honest in my assessment of the games and individual players.

Why do you think you were such a successful partnership on the radio with Boro commentator Alastair Brownlee? After all, you won awards.

BERNIE

The reason the partnership worked was we were totally different. Ally would see and say no wrong and I would just say it as it was. The one thing we had in common was we were both passionate and loved doing the commentary.
In 10 years working together we never missed one pre-season, league, FA Cup or Carling Cup game. I missed two UEFA Cup games due to my phobia of flying.
When we were doing the commentary we had record figures on match days of around 70,000 listeners.
It wasn't just the football, there was a fun element as well with the phone-in afterwards. It was always lively, to say the least.
To confirm that we were a half decent commentary team we were nominated for a New York Radio Festival award. Both of us flew to the States and came away with a gold award.
We were both delighted with that, but at the end of that season we were flabbergasted when we lost the commentary rights.

Many people thought you lost the commentary because you can be so outspoken. What are your own thoughts on that situation and do you think in hindsight that you might have been too critical?

BERNIE

Was it the right thing to do? No. Everyone lost out and the fans lost a smashing partnership which the figures confirmed they enjoyed listening to. Ally of course has continued to do the commentary on the BBC with my former Boro team-mate Gary Gill. Is it on a par with myself and Ally? Absolutely not. I honestly believe that if clubs could get away with gagging the fans' opinions and stop phone-ins and other public forums, they would. They want your money but they don't want you to have an opinion. I always say in my defence that my opinion has never cost the club three points or got us relegated. If it did, I would maybe stop. There were conflicting stories as to why we lost the commentary and some blamed me for my outspoken comments. If I was to blame, why did it take 10 years to do it? After all, I had never changed as a pundit.

I have always had strong opinions and was never afraid to air them. What I do know is when we weren't given the rights, the amount of letters, e-mails, texts and callers defending us was unbelievable.

You and Alastair were good friends. How has that friendship held up since you parted company on the radio?

BERNIE

We don't phone each other and very seldom bump into each other. Both of us have just gone our own way, but life goes on.

Why haven't you put your money where your mouth is and got a job in football as a coach or manager?

BERNIE

I did my prelim badge years ago. I followed that up and got my UEFA B badge in 1999 and my plan was to go and do my A Licence. But I was disillusioned with the whole set-up. I enjoyed the practical side but not the theory.

My dad has been at me for years to get my full badge and to get into coaching or management.

If someone offered me a job like Gareth Southgate got the Middlesbrough job, I would go out and get my A Licence in a flash. I know there are plenty of people with their full badge who haven't got a job in the game though. The whole thing in my opinion is a money spinner.

Tell us about your fear of flying. Has that cost you jobs over the years? Are you over it now?

BERNIE

There is no denying that my phobia has got in the way. I have avoided holidays to Bermuda, Cyprus and Spain because of it. I have backed out of international games and I have had opportunities to play in China and America that I have missed. I have also lost a lot of money because of my fear of the steel bird. Up until the Lockerbie disaster, I loved flying. But I passed the disaster site the following day and that picture lives in my memory. Over the years I have flown to places like Hong Kong and Singapore. I'm not saying I'm Biggles now, but I'm improving.I don't drink, so can't disguise my fear with alcohol. But I have been know to pop valium. Sometimes I've been higher than the plane itself. But over the last few years I have weaned off the tablets and managed to travel to several European destinations cleaner than Kerry Katona.

Describe your current relationship with Middlesbrough Football Club.

BERNIE

Since joining the media my relationship with them has never been good, and since losing the commentary it's virtually non-existent. The number of people who have asked me if I'm banned from the Riverside is staggering. I would like to put this straight once and for all. For me to do my radio show from the Riverside, it would mean me plugging in what they call an

ISDN box, so that I could link in with the studio and the people of the North East. The way I look at it, I am piggy in the middle. The club want a few quid from the radio station for me to do the gig and the radio don't want to pay the asking amount.

It's purely a commercial decision. I had that clarified to my face by Boro chairman Steve Gibson a couple of years back.

You've been on Teesside now for 25 years. Why have you stayed in the area?

BERNIE

I have stayed in the area after my football career because I love it. I love the people, the fantastic countryside and obviously I'm heavily involved with Real Radio on the Three Legends show. Both of my sons are born and bred in Middlesbrough as well. But the biggest thing that I enjoy is there is no bigotry.

It's a more enjoyable way of life. Don't get me wrong, I love Glasgow, my parents, and my mates live up there.

It's a terrific city and I enjoy going up there to visit, but Teesside is my home. The only down side to living down here is my boys support England and wear England shirts and stand up for the national anthem!

You've been on the Three Legends show for over a decade - now with Micky Horswill and Malcolm Macdonald. How has that time been for you?

BERNIE

It's now 11 years since the Legends show started and in that time we have received record listening figures. I absolutely love it. The banter, the callers and having an opinion, and the fans make the show. At the start it was just a phone-in but now we are inundated with e-mails and texts, as well as callers.

The original line up was Malcolm Macdonald, ex-Newcastle, Eric Gates, ex-Sunderland, and myself.
Sunderland's FA Cup winner Micky Horswill replaced Eric Gates after seven years, but although the line-up has changed the chemistry hasn't. Malcolm is like the headmaster who comes over as well educated and polite, and me and Micky are like the naughty schoolkids who enjoy a bit of banter and laugh at anything. The range of calls and callers we get is unbelievable.

How is Bernie Slaven in 2011 and what does the future hold?

BERNIE

I still thoroughly enjoy the Legends show, and me and Micky are looking to start our own soccer school. The three of us do the odd Legends evening live at social clubs as well.
Regarding the future, I hope to remain in the media side of things for years to come.

What are your thoughts on the Boro at the moment? It's been an incredible period in the club's history with FA Cup, Carling Cup and UEFA Cup Finals - now they are fighting for Championship survival.

BERNIE

It's incredible how things have gone downhill since 2006, and everyone involved must carry the can. There is no denying winning the Carling Cup in 2004 was, to use Steve McClaren's words, magnificent. It was our first trophy in 128 years and it was a magical occasion.
We have attracted some amazing players over the years like Junninho, Ravanelli, Emerson, Barmby, Merson and Ziege, but unfortunately those players have long gone.

The players that have come in have been inferior, but to be fair to chairman Steve Gibson, he has done a magnificent job over the years. He delivered everything he said he would - a new stadium, new training facilities, big name players and that elusive first trophy.

But since the UEFA Cup Final we have been on a downward spiral and have tried everything to address the problems.

We parted ways with Gareth Southgate and Gordon Strachan as managers and coaches and players have left.

The only thing that hasn't changed is the chairman and the chief executive, and in my opinion it's time to make a change at the top and get some fresh investment.

Other than that I can't see how we are going to get back into the Premier League.We started the 2010/11 season as favourites with the bookmakers to win the Championship and after buying in Scotland's so-called elite with Strachan at the helm I was fairly confident. How wrong was I? Apart from Barry Robson, the Scottish players haven't performed and Strachan got it horribly wrong on and off the park. He came over as rude, arrogant and obnoxious in interviews. Jose Mourinho gets away with things because he is charismatic. Strachan was charmless. My old Boro team-mate Tony Mowbray has now take over of course and I hope he turns it around for us

HONOURS

BERNARD JOSEPH SLAVEN

PLAYING CAREER HISTORY

1981-1983 Morton
1983-1985 Albion Rovers
1985-1992 Middlesbrough
1992-1994 Port vale
1994-1995 Darlington.

PLAYING CAREER HONOURS (Winners)

Port vale
1993   Auto Glass Trophy.

CAPS 7 full caps for Republic of Ireland.

Member of the world cup squad 1990.

First goal for Middlesbrough against Bradford.

In action, during a premier league game at Ayresome park.

"I loved my time there, my problem was with an individual, which was sad."

Viduka on why he left Middlesbrough.

MARK VIDUKA
MIDDLESBROUGH

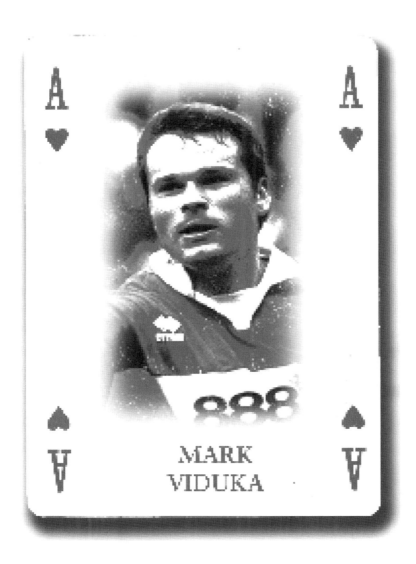

MARK VIDUKA

Mark Anthony Viduka was born in Melbourne, Australia on October 9, 1975. He arrived on Teesside from Leeds for a fee of £3 million before departing for Newcastle in the summer of 2007. His qualities are an immaculate first touch, he is great at holding the ball up, has good body strength, scores and creates goals and brings team-mates into play - a very talented and skillful player all round.

I travelled to the Newcastle training ground in Benton to interview Viduka. It was February and the snow was four inches deep, with blizzard conditions.

As I jumped out of the car, I headed for the main reception only to be told by several Newcastle employees that the interview was taking place elsewhere. I was directed back out into the Arctic conditions, went right and right again only to find myself at the back of the building.

There was a massive glass window and the first person I clapped eyes on was caretaker manager Chris Hughton, who I knew from my Ireland days.

He looked in disbelief and shouted: "Come around the front to the reception."

It was then I knew I had been stitched up - Geordie bastards!

I did the interview with the Duke in a small room. I found him warm, straight and funny.

On the way out I had a word with Chris Hughton, who said: "You did well

getting Viduka, he's a complex character."

BERNIE

You were born in Melbourne, Australia, but are also of Croatian and Ukrainian descent?

MARK

To be honest my parents were both from Croatia but they emigrated to Australia in the 60s, in 1964. My dad's from an area in Croatia which is called Dalmatia. It's on the coastline. And my mums from Bosnia, but she lived in a place called Slovenia, but her background is Ukrainian. So it's quite complicated. She's from the ex-Yugoslavia but her generations were Ukrainian, you know what I mean? But my dad was Croatian.

BERNIE

Could you have played international football for the Ukraine or Croatia?

MARK

Probably not the Ukraine because that's sort of like, down the lines. For example, my mothers grandparents moved from Ukraine to the ex-Yugoslavia. Her and her mother were born in Croatia or Yugoslavia. At the time I could have played for Croatia though.

BERNIE
You started your career with Melbourne Knights in 1993. What kind of standard was that?

MARK

Well it was semi-professional at the time. I was professional -
most of the players were semi. Most of them had jobs and they'd
do that on the side. The standard wasn't too bad to be honest.
We had quite a good league at the time, very competitive. Some
very good players came out of that league.

BERNIE

A couple of years later you moved to Croatia Zagreb, now called
Dinamo Zagreb. How did you enjoy your time there?

MARK

It was mixed. It was good and it was different. It was a big
difference for me having lived in Australia, which is a
democracy. At the time I moved it was war time there, so
everything was chaos at the time. Half the country was occupied
and stuff like that. They won the territory back, there was a lot
of political problems but I enjoyed the time there. I liked
learning about my background a little bit more. I mean, I won
four league titles, I won three cups and played in the Champions
League, I played in the UEFA Cup.
So it was a great stepping stone for me, a great, great
experience.

BERNIE

Looking back, is it true that Melbourne Knights named one of
the stands The Mark Viduka Stand?

MARK

It is, yeah (Laughs). To be honest I was overseas, I don't know why.

BERNIE

Were you that good?

MARK

(Laughs). Well for two years in a row, I was named Australia's player of the year. I was top goal scorer, player of the year and Under-21 player of the year. I won everything that you could win in Australia and we won the league for the first time as well in the history of the club. I think I wasn't bad.

BERNIE

In 1998 you left Zagreb and joined my boyhood heroes Glasgow Celtic for £3.5 million. A month after signing Celtic announced you had quit the club. What was that all about?

MARK

What happened was Bernie, it was towards the last three or four months of my time in Croatia. I had a bad time, I had a very difficult time with the fans, with the club and the press, I had big problems with that. When I came to Glasgow it was in the winter transfer window, it was 98 going on to 99 and I came then and I went to Joe Vengloss at the time and I said to him: "I need a bit of a break, I've had a hard time there." I just wanted to have a bit of a break and then come back and start again. That was basically it.

BERNIE

As clean cut as that?

MARK

Once the press got wind of it, it wasn't clean cut.

BERNIE

In your first full season in Glasgow you were voted Scottish player of the year and scored 27 goals. You must have been delighted?

MARK

Well yeah, I was very happy. After the difficult start I had there was a lot of negative press about me. There was a lot of rumours made up which were all untrue really. I can't remember all of them but 99.9 per cent were untrue. There were stories of me going to a mental hospital, there was everything, and I was really determined to prove everybody wrong.

BERNIE

You were on the receiving end of a bit of stick from the Celtic supporters after you claimed to be only playing at about 75 per cent of your capability. Why did you say that?

MARK

I didn't say that. No, see what happened, I went to Leeds then I think an article came out in the Scottish newspapers saying that I had said that I played at 75 per cent in games, which I never

have. Whoever got that article or whatever I would love them to show it to me because I never said
that to anybody. You can't if you're playing 75 per cent, it doesn't matter what league you're playing or whatever, you can't be voted player of the year if you're playing at 75 per cent and be a top goal scorer.

BERNIE

Ex-Arsenal player Ian Wright claimed that during half time in Celtic's Scottish cup defeat against Inverness Caledonian, that an unnamed striker refused to go back out for the second half. Was that you? If so, why?

MARK

You've got all that stuff off Wikipedia! (Laughs)

BERNIE

Yes, I saw it on Wikipedia. Was it you? Because he didn't name you, did he?

MARK

I don't know which striker he's talking about because there was a bit of a ruckus going off in the dressing room at the time.
So there were a few players that were a little bit upset at the time because we were losing at half-time to Inverness in the Scottish FA Cup and nobody was in a good mood, put it that way. Nobody likes to be losing.

BERNIE

So there were a number of candidates, not just you? He could have been talking about a number of centre forwards?

MARK

I was the only one who didn't come out but yeah, it was me yeah.

BERNIE

You left Celtic and joined Leeds for a fee of £6million. How did you enjoy your time at Elland Road?

MARK

It was excellent, really good at Leeds. We had a great environment, great atmosphere, we got to the semi-final of the Champions League and I think we finished fourth or fifth in the league at the time. It was just a great atmosphere, good times and really positive. We had good players and I loved it, I really loved it.

BERNIE

In your first season you scored 22 goals, including four against Liverpool in a memorable 4-3 victory. That must have been a highlight?

MARK

Yes, definitely. I mean, that game is a game were everything went right. Basically I remember saying in an interview after the game that I didn't play exceptionally well but I got four chances and I put them away. I've played in games where I've played unbelievably, took on players and set up chances and did all these great moves and whatever but I never got on the goal scoring sheets. But in this game it was one where, you know, four times the ball came to me in positions and I finished them.

BERNIE

As a striker what would you rather do - have a great game or score goals?

MARK

See I'm a little bit different, I'm a little bit picky probably, a little bit of a perfectionist. A lot of times people say just shoot, just score, but I like a little bit of finesse - that's what fuels me. I remember one of the best games I ever played for Leeds was when we played in the Champions League against Lazio away and Alan Smith scored and we won 1-0. I set him up with a back heel and it was a beautiful move. It was one of the best games I've ever played in. So if somebody said to me four goals against Liverpool and that game, I think they are on a par.

BERNIE

Unusual for a striker - I just wanted to score. (Duke laughs) After a couple of years with Leeds the club hit off-the-field financial troubles and started selling their key players. Could you believe that after Champions League football the club was struggling?

MARK

It was devastating for everybody who was involved in the club.

We were in administration for a while, you're in the club and you know what it's like, you get used to the kit people, you're friends with the people in the kitchen, you're friends with everybody, the cleaners. And you get to know everybody and everybody was just unsure of their jobs, nobody knew what was going on. Whether the club would be bought, whether the club wouldn't be bought. It was just a big shame really, it was very difficult to take as a player and also as a person who was working at the club at the time.

BERNIE

You joined the Leeds exodus and signed for Middlesbrough - why Middlesbrough?

MARK

What are you laughing at?

BERNIE

I have to ask the question

MARK

Well at the time they were very interested in signing me and it was a good option for me because I had lived in that same place for four or five years at the time.

BERNIE

Where was that, Harrogate?

MARK

In Linton, which is Wetherby. They made a good offer for me,
they approached me and it looked like they really wanted me.
Steve McClaren at the time was a good manager and I was on
my holidays and Keith Lamb came out to see me.
It was really nice, it was a good move for me, you know?

BERNIE

Your debut season at the Riverside was impressive but disrupted
by injuries. Was that frustrating?

MARK

Yes, I mean it's always frustrating. The first season was my
worst season at Middlesbrough. If I look back nobody likes to
be injured, everyone likes to be playing.

BERNIE

On the subject of injuries, the critics would say you're injury
prone. Do you agree or disagree with that?

MARK

I disagree

BERNIE

Why would you disagree?

MARK

I disagree because for 10 years I hardly ever had any injuries.
I played for Melbourne Knights, Dinamo Zagreb, I played for
Leeds almost every game, I played for Celtic almost every game
as well. Once I got to Middlesbrough a little bit less, but for
many years, I mean you get players who get injured at 19 or 20-
years-old and it takes them two or three years to get over it. For
example look at Jonathan Woodgate - he's had a very hard time
with injuries. But for a good 10 years before I even came to this
country as well I was playing every game.
BERNIE.

I mean, it's a bit of a myth because until I looked it up, I was
astonished at the amount of games you've played and the goals
you've scored as well is second to none.
But there is a myth that goes about that Mark Viduka is always
injured.

MARK

Yes, because as you get older you get more prone to injury don't
you? And after playing that many games and training sessions
and whatever it takes its toll after a little while. But because it's
now they want you to be playing and that's the case usually.
In football people have short memories, you know?

BERNIE

In the 2005/6 season you were in sensational form in all
competitions for Middlesbrough. What happened in the UEFA
Cup final against Seville?

MARK

The UEFA Cup final was a big, big disappointment. It's all well
and good saying we got to the final. Yeah, we did get to the final
in a very unbelievable way. That lead up to that final will remain
something, that's the best memories of my football career.
It was ridiculous the way we got into that final. That final for
three weeks after I was a wreck, because I wanted to win -
everybody wanted to win. I remember after that final I had to go
and play in the Confederations Cup and I just remember I was
devastated for three weeks after. But I had to pick myself up
because first of all I was disappointed in myself. I had a good
chance to score a goal and the goalkeeper saved it.
Also, obviously, there was a penalty decision that should have
been given and things didn't go the way we would have liked
and we didn't play particularly well.

BERNIE

Leading up to that final you were rested along with two other
players. Was that your decision?

MARK

No, no. The reason I was left out was because I had played
against West Ham and either had got a knock or a calf strain.
That was the reason why I wasn't playing, because I was rested.

BERNIE

Throughout your career you've worn the number nine jersey.
Are you superstitious?

MARK

Not really. At the minute I'm 36. I had 36 at Celtic - I was either 9, 10 or 36.
I don't know why when I got to Celtic that was halfway through the season. That was the number that was free - 36.
So I had no option. Six and three adds up to nine. I don't know.
(Laughs)

BERNIE

Have you any superstitions?

MARK

Not really, no. I'm not superstitious at all.

BERNIE

You played alongside Gareth Southgate. Did he portray leadership qualities in terms of becoming a manager?

MARK

Yes, I think for Gareth, for me it was a natural progression for him to go into management. He's that type of person I think. First of all he's very well respected in footballers' eyes, everybody liked him. He has got those people skills, he's a genuine type of person, he's not going to go behind your back trying to do things.

BERNIE

A lot of them do.

MARK

Some of them do. He did have the qualities, yes.

BERNIE

In your third and final season for Middlesbrough you scored 19 goals and Gareth expressed his interest in keeping you. Why did you leave?
(MARK laughs)

BERNIE

Come on, why did you go?

MARK

Well because, the reason why I left was it was Christmas time, I had six months to go on my contract which is four months of the season. No-one had come to me with an offer. They said: "When we get safe from relegation, we'll make you an offer."
In the mean time we kept playing, I was playing very well, I was scoring a lot of goals towards the end of the season, doing really well, and still nobody had come to me. The first offer I received from them was when I was on holiday, so no-one had said anything to me. Other clubs started to show an interest, there were seven or eight clubs who were already showing that they wanted me to go to their teams and I'd got no response at all from Middlesbrough. It was like, not even an offer. Listen, they made me an offer - I don't even recall how much it was. It was the same money that I was on and I was a free agent at the end of the season. The other clubs were showing a lot of interest in me. I was on my holidays and they sent me an offer by mail here to England. When I came back I didn't even know that they had made me a better offer, they sent it by mail in my post.

When I came back to England I had already signed for
Newcastle. I opened up my mail box and there's an offer from
Middlesbrough. So it's just the way that they treated that whole
matter.
It was like, you're our player, you have to sign for us, you
understand?

BERNIE

Yes.

MARK

As I had other clubs, other managers who were desperate to
ring, I know Gareth wanted me to stay, I liked Middlesbrough, I
loved being there, it was ideal for me. I had been there for three
years, I enjoyed the fans, I had a great relationship with the fans,
I had my house that I have lived in for seven years.
I was in the same house, my kids were starting school, it was
ideal for me.

BERNIE

On the last day of the season against Fulham I walked past you
and the chief executive Keith Lamb on the stairway. Was Keith
trying to drag you into a room to sign?

MARK

Sort of, yes. And I had said to him at that moment, you can ask
him yourself, I said to him: "It's a disgrace the way you treat
your players." Sometimes it doesn't have to be money, it doesn't
have to be money, do you understand?
If you feel that they appreciate you, it's the same as every job.
You know, you've been a footballer.

If they say to you: "Don't worry Duke, we'll look after you, you've done a good job for us, we'll look after you."
But nobody contacted me or my agent or whatever for months. For months the end of the season was coming and they knew that I was free. Then they expected me to sign it, almost as if they don't want you to sign but they do. You don't even know. So I had to make a decision whether or not I'm going to.
I couldn't make a decision at Christmas time when legally I could have signed for somebody, which I didn't because I was waiting for them coming with a decent offer.
The first offer they made me was the same money I was on and I was a free agent. It doesn't make sense.

BERNIE

What was Steve McClaren like?

MARK

Steve McClaren, I think tactically he was good. On the field, coaching and organising the team and stuff like that.
I think his man management skills were his weakest point. That was his first managerial job and it takes time.
I look at Gareth and I think: "F**k, that's a hard job."
Playing with a team and then becoming manager - very, very difficult. I personally don't think I could have done that, which is a big, big thing for him because you've played as mates, you've done things together and all of a sudden you're the boss.
Very difficult.

BERNIE
McClaren got the England job, where you surprised?

MARK

Was I surprised? Well, we did really well in the UEFA Cup and they were desperate for a new manager, people were calling out for an English manager. I wasn't really surprised, no. I remember Steve Harrison was making jokes all the time about that after the UEFA Cup final.

BERNIE

I thought the timing was awful. Did McClaren have to announce the England job before the UEFA Cup final?

MARK

Awful, no. It's awful when you get beaten 4-0, you look for excuses. But if we would have won nobody would have said anything.

BERNIE

That's true. (Laughs)

MARK

Someone would have said: "He was going to England anyway, he didn't give a shit."

BERNIE

Yes, you can't win either way.

BERNIE

When you left the Riverside one or two people criticised you, saying you never played enough games or scored enough goals. What would you say to that? You must have read the articles criticising you?

MARK

I was very disappointed, very disappointed.

BERNIE

What contact did you have with the chairman before you left?

MARK

He rang me when I was in Australia. I was in the car park.

BERNIE

Were you eating an ice cream?

MARK

I was in the car park.

BERNIE

You weren't dogging were you?

MARK

I wasn't dogging (Laughs).

103

I was in the car park.

I remember that conversation and I told him the exact reason why I'm not going to re-sign, because at the last minute they made me a ridiculous offer. They wanted to make me the highest paid player in the club's history and whatever.

I told him that the reason why I'm not going to sign, and it was because of the fact of, the way I was treated.

They weren't f*****g getting a whip out but its those things. Football is a different business from any other business it's not the same as running a factory, its not the same as running his businesses or whatever. Footballers are specific people I think and that's probably how they get to that level.

If it was that easy every man and his dog would be a footballer. So to get to that level you have to have something in you. But most players just want, as I have said earlier its not always about the money. He offered me to be the highest paid player in Middlesbrough's history but I told him it's not about the money it's the way they treat you. Okay, for example Xavier had an offer from America. He had an offer for here, he had an offer from there. He wanted to keep him but he had offers from other clubs, whatever. Middlesbrough said nothing not even a 'well done, you did a good job for us'. It's the way sometimes. It's not about the money, it's the way you feel wanted to stay.

I felt when I was leaving that they were saying: "Yeah, take it or leave it," you know what I mean?

Now if I've got a better offer or the same offer somewhere else you'd say: "If you're doing that to me why would I want to stay with you?" Do you understand?

And that was the reason. I told Steve Gibson the only reason is that. The first season I signed where I scored 21 he comes out in the national papers saying it was all about the money for me.

Now that's a disappointment because he knows the conversation we had, whether it's about the money its my business.

If you're working in a factory and another factory asks you to do the same job for 200 quid more an hour you're going to say:

"Look, I like your factory here but they want me more than what you want me." You understand? And you ask any punter out there or any normal person who's in that same predicament, they'd say: "Look, my family needs more money, I'll go with these guys." It's the same thing.
It's not that we need f*****g
people waving fans in our faces or giving us f*****g grapes.
No, it's just decent everyday respect.
Football is different because without these players to perform the club goes down. That's were the revenue comes from isn't it? If you're not in the Premiership.

BERNIE

Is it not the manager's job to deal with contractual stuff?
In that situation I would be going and fighting on your behalf if I was a manager.

MARK

Gareth probably was and I know he wanted to keep me.
He definitely wanted to keep me. Whether he did or didn't I still respect Gareth as a person and as a manager as well.

BERNIE

Did you enjoy your time at the Riverside?

MARK

I did, I loved it. I'll remember some fantastic games, especially in Europe and that's how I will remember Middlesbrough.
I loved the time there. My problem was with an individual it's sad as a representative of the club.
But I had a good time. I made good friends at the club, as I said.

The kit lady Elaine and all the people who worked at the club, they were very nice people. I enjoyed coming to work there.

BERNIE

Did you ever see Bill Beswick?

MARK

I spoke to Bill a few times, that's when Steve McClaren was there, but not too often.
I went in now and again and he did everybody, he took the whole team for session.

BERNIE

You joined North-east rivals Newcastle on a free transfer. How did that move come about?

MARK

They were desperate for me to come. I had a choice of four clubs and Big Sam (Allardyce) was desperate for me to come and I thought he'd bring a bit of stability to the club long-term. He'd done a great job at Bolton and like everybody thought he'd be there long-term and that was that.

BERNIE

Could you believe it when he left? You were his first signing.

MARK

I didn't think it would be that quick. I thought it was a long term kind of thing but as soon as he signed a new owner came in as well who had their own thoughts on the team and ideas. It was a funny sort of a situation.

BERNIE

You scored your first Newcastle goal against Middlesbrough. How sweet was that?

MARK

Well it was sweet when it hit the back of the net.

BERNIE

What did you think of when you hit the net? Who did you think of?

MARK

No, no. Listen, I don't hold any grudges, I've got nothing against Keith Lamb either. There's no doubting he was the biggest reason why I left but I've nothing against him. I like Steve Gibson, I think he's done really well for the club. I think he's done a good job keeping them in the Premier league and it's not an easy job keeping a club like Middlesbrough in the top flight. It hasn't got the revenue of a Newcastle or a Chelsea. It's not an easy job and I understand they have to do that and I respect them, it's just that I was a little bit disappointed with Steve Gibson. Because I had the vision of somebody who wouldn't do that, I've had those sort of instances in the past where managers are under pressure, then they go and blame it on a player to deflect it from themselves. I didn't expect Steve Gibson to do something like that. I know it was a difficult situation for him because he lost one of his best strikers to the rivals and maybe he had to make the club look good and himself look good with the way he came out with that. But it was still disappointing.

BERNIE

Could you believe both you and Yakubu left?

MARK

Yes, I could because of the reasons I just told you.
Well, let's look. Why did Woody go? Why does Stewie Downing want to go?
Stewie's a great player, one of the best players I've played with definitely as a striker. He set up many goals for me and for other players. He is a very good player and he loves that club, he was born there, he lives there. But... (Shrugs his shoulders)

BERNIE

Keegan comes across as charismatic, was he?

MARK

He was charismatic, he was good. I liked Kevin because he loves pure football and I love pure football. We got on really well to be honest. I liked him, I really did.

BERNIE

Keegan changed the formation to 4-3-3, with you, Michael Owen and Martins up front. Which formation do you prefer?

MARK

Oh, I loved it. That was my best period for sure. I really liked that, you know? I wasn't sure whether or not it would have worked at first with the three of us but we were unbelievable. We played some really good games and we felt confident as a group going into those games.

BERNIE

What about lone striker - do you like that role?

MARK

I don't like that, I prefer to play with somebody. When you play up front it's much easier for the defenders to defend against you because they can put one on you and let one drop off a little bit. If you have somebody else like a Yakubu or whatever, two up front, at least you're taking one player away from you and if you get the ball and turn around you can see somebody else. Whereas when I was younger I was a little better, quicker. (Laughs). But as you get older your pace disappears and you need someone to play off I think anyway.

BERNIE

Keegan walked out and Joe Kinnear filled in. What has your relationship with Joe been like?

MARK

Yeah, good. He seems like a decent bloke, I've had no problems with him at all. He keeps himself to himself, he's a quiet type of a person.

BERNIE

Reading the reports, he's far from quiet! (Laughs)

MARK

Oh, to you guys he's different (laughs) but to the players he's a decent guy.

BERNIE

Obviously Joe has a heart problem at the minute.
MARK

I wish... Listen, these things are more important than any football game, people's health and I wish him and his family all the best.

BERNIE

Off the field the club has been put up for sale by Mike Ashley, the owner. Do off-the-field things affect the players?

MARK

Well, you like to say that it shouldn't but it does. Like it or not, it does. I mean, it's just the stability and the instability of the whole thing. Every day you read something else and nobody knows whether... You look at the Man Uniteds, the Arsenals and the Chelseas, you've got Sir Alex Ferguson, sir Alex has been there for 100 years. (Laughs) And that is the reason why they are so successful. That is the reason they are always stable. If you look at how many managers this club has had in the last I don't know how many years, it can't be a good thing.

BERNIE

Looking back at Middlesbrough, they are second bottom of the Premier League as we speak. Can they escape relegation with 13 games left?

MARK

Can they do it? Of course. I think to be honest I'm surprised at the situation how it is now because the way that they started off the season was very good. I mean, 13 games ago they were flying. They were doing very well, playing some good football. They have brought in some good players as well.

BERNIE

In my opinion we let yourself Yakubu, Cattermole and Young go and brought in inferior players.

MARK

You brought in Tuncay.

BERNIE

I would pay to watch him - a good finisher.

MARK

But up front Alves, he's alright. Wheats has stepped up and done well.

BERNIE

But you still think we'll get out of it?

111

MARK

I hope so.

BERNIE

Would you put your money on it?

MARK

I don't gamble mate. (Laughs)

BERNIE

You've gained 43 full caps for Australia. Was captaining your country in the 2006 World Cup the highlight?

MARK

It was unbelievable. You know, it was the second World Cup we played in and it was just something special, unforgettable to be honest. I was watching pictures last night of my family which we took in the World Cup. My kids, all my family came from Australia and stayed in Germany. The way that the tournament was organised was unbelievable. The Germans did such a good job over there, we had such a great time and played some big teams. We played Croatia obviously, who are close to me and we got through to the next round. It was very disappointing, again the same thing as the UEFA Cup final. It took me three weeks to recover. I didn't want to watch the rest of the
World Cup after we got kicked out in that manner.
If you remember the game, Italy got a penalty in the last second of the game against us.
Do you remember that? It was definitely not a penalty and very

disappointing. After that, just the whole experience was unbelievable.

BERNIE

Your career highlights are what?

MARK

The high point would have to be the World Cup and also there have been plenty.

BERNIE

More highs than lows?

MARK

Oh, there has been a lot of lows mate.

BERNIE

Give us some of them.

MARK

Lows would be getting booed off personally in front of 40,000 of my own fans in Croatia. Scoring a goal away from home getting abused by the fans in Croatia, very low points.
The low point was when I went to Celtic. At first when I went back home it was a very difficult time for me to get through.
The high points, I'll tell you something.
We got a bottle of scotch. I won Scottish player of the year and top scorer and I went home and got a bottle of scotch, nice Scottish whisky. And I just sat there on the couch, a rented

couch (laughs) and started drinking it. I was so happy at that moment, very happy, and then somebody goes and writes I only gave 75 per cent of my capabilities. Oh, a big high point as well was winning the title with Melbourne Knights.
That was the biggest thing.

BERNIE

As it stands today, you have played in 489 games and scored 237 goals. More to come?

MARK

I hope so mate.

BERNIE

There was recently talk that you could retire. Is that true?

MARK

I don't know, I don't like being injured. I love playing and for me I would rather somebody pulled out my tooth without an anesthetic than go on a f*****g tread mill every day or in a weights room or something like that.
I love the ball, I love playing and if I cant do that properly... This year has been a big testing year for me because I haven't been able to do what I love doing. You know yourself, players who love physically playing that love running all day, they're players that love to play. If they loved strength work they'd be in the gym all day. I just love the ball, that's all. It's a good habit.
I'm not physical, I'm not one who loves running obviously! (Laughs)

BERNIE

I've noticed.

MARK

I don't mind a bit of gym work, I love doing something. I love setting up players, I love scoring goals, I love anything to do with the ball and when that's taken away from me it's no fun. So this year has been a really testing year for me. I'll have to see.

BERNIE

How long is your contract?

MARK

I'm finished at the end of this season.

BERNIE

How old are you now?

MARK

33

BERNIE

A couple of years if you want it left?

MARK

Maybe, I don't want to be playing if I'm in the physio room.

BERNIE

And when you retire in years to come will you retire in England or Australia?

MARK

Probably Australia.

BERNIE

Have you been able to get a bond with the Newcastle fans?

MARK

Well listen, I think that while I've played I've probably done quite well. Last year I went through a patch when I did quite well and I combined well. Obviously it's frustrating for the fans and frustrating for me, especially now we have a lot of injuries. They want to see you playing and I want to see me playing as well. To be honest, they've been very supportive of me. There's 50,000 people at a game and not everyone's going to have the same opinion. They are entitled to love me or hate me but in general they have been very good.

BERNIE

Duke, thanks very much.

MARK

No problem, Bernie.

HONOURS

MARK VIDUKA

PLAYING CAREER

1993-1995 Melbourne Knights
1995-1998 Dinamo Zagreb
1998-2000 Celtic
2000-2004 Leeds Utd
2004-2007 Middlesbrough
2007-present Newcastle

PLAYING HONOURS

Melbourne Knights
1994-95 NSL title

Zagreb

1995 League
1995 Cup
1996 League
1996 Cup
1997 League
1997 Cup

CAPS 43 full caps for Australia

Viduka playing for Middlesbrough.

In action for Newcastle

"I HAD PLAYED FOR ENGLAND,
I HAD PLAYED FOR TEAMS THAT HAD
PLAYED ALL OVER EUROPE,
MY QUALIFICATIONS WERE NOT IN
QUESTION, MAYBE IT WAS JUST ME,
MY PERSONALITY."

Jack on why he didn't get the England job.

JACK CHARLTON
NEWCASTLE

JACK
CHARLTON

Jack was born in Ashington, Northumberland on May 8ᵗʰ 1935, as a player he notched up a record 629 league games for Leeds United between 1953 and 1973. On his retirement Jack expressed an interest in league management and was offered the job at Middlesbrough and accepted the post on May 7ᵗʰ 1973. I met up with Jack at his home in the outskirts of Newcastle. Jack was charming, funny, and ruthless; he was the only manager that had the happy medium. By that I mean, he could mix with the lads for a laugh and a drink and a sing song, but during training sessions or a match day he was the boss no one dare stand on his toes.

I recall a scene which I had never witnessed before during a training session, it was during Italia 1990 World Cup. It was an eleven verses eleven game, up front for the first team eleven was John Aldridge and Tony Cascirino, from the start of the practice game Jack was on Cascirinos case. Cas get your touch right, Cas head the bloody ball, Cas hold the dam ball up, Jack snapped and shouted Cas if you don't get yourself sorted your out. Five minutes later Cas was out and Niall Quinn replaced him, not just for training but for the fourth coming World Cup game against Holland.

In all my career I have never witnessed a manager dropping a first team regular because of a poor training session. Rightly or wrongly Jack proved who was boss.

Big Jack is one of the loveliest guys I have ever met, he's a straight talker with no airs and graces, what you see is what you get.

Before the interview big Jack demanded I bought him fish and chips, it's not everyday you sit down to eat fish and chips with a World Cup winner, I felt honoured.

JACK

Listen Bernie, before we start, do you still talk to the dog on the phone?

BERNIE

I told you not to mention that, of course I do!

JACK

Well, I was a little bit perturbed at you showing your arse on television by the way - my players don't do that!

BERNIE

I apologise Jack. You started your playing career at Leeds United. Were you a bit disappointed that it wasn't with Newcastle? You must have been a Newcastle fan as a youngster ?

JACK

No, nobody wanted to play for Newcastle at that time and our mother wouldn't allow us to play for Newcastle.
At that time they wanted our kid (Bobby) to go, and they wanted me to go for trials and things like that.
But back then it wasn't all straightforward and I got an offer to go to Leeds for a trial and decided to go there.

BERNIE

You spent 22 years at Elland Road. How did you last so long?

JACK

I went at 15 and became a ground staff boy, as they called them in those days. Not an apprentice, a ground staff boy. You did your work on the ground, you worked in the dressing rooms and you cleaned boots and the toilets and you did all the jobs.

BERNIE

You had me doing that with Ireland!

JACK

Now and again. Then I had a year at 17 when I signed professional terms, then I had a year when I played in the first team, one game, then for the reserves in the Yorkshire league.Then you had a two-year period when everyone had to go in the army.So I didn't really pick up playing football professionally until I came out of the army at the age of 20. Then I went straight into the first team at Leeds and I was in there for the rest of the time until I was 38.

BERNIE

You started off as a full-back, is that right?

JACK

I went and had a trial as a full-back, yeah. I had never played centre-back.I probably wasn't good enough to be a centre-back, because full-backs were always the bad players in those days.When you decided to pick a team, the last ones to get picked were the full-backs.So I started as a full-back, then very quickly they moved me to centre-back at Leeds and that's where I played for the rest of my career.

BERNIE

What were your greatest achievements at Leeds?

JACK

Oh, I don't know, just being there for 22 years and being with Don Revie for 10, 11 years when we didn't win as much as we should have done.But we competed so much in every competition that we were always involved in the league, cups and Europe.You played between 65 and 70 games a year, mainly at the end of a season when things became frantic.Because the season finished, then before the cup finals your games had to be out of the way, then the final was at the beginning of May.It really was very difficult to focus when all you're doing is playing important game after important game right the way through until the end of the season, two and three games a week. We didn't win as much as we should. The year we sort of opted out or got out of the other competitions, we went on to win the championship no problem.

BERNIE

Leeds had the reputation of being a dirty side. Would you agree with that?

JACK

No, you can't say a dirty side. We had a couple of players that could look after themselves and caused us a bit of aggravation sometimes.I mean, I've yelled at my own players for some of the things they did.We had a bit of a reputation when we first came into the division in 1965,when we got promoted and we got to the cup final against Liverpool.

Things started to change over the next few years, then people suddenly realised that Leeds United weren't a dirty side.
They could look after themselves, but they were also a very, very good side.In fact, one of the best sides people said that this country produced for a long, long time.

BERNIE

Is that up until you met Celtic?

JACK

Yeah, well, Celtic beat us in the semi-final of the European Cup. That's the only thing I didn't win at Leeds. I never won a European Cup winners' medal. We got beaten by Celtic and beaten by Hamburg, the German side.

BERNIE

In 1966 you were a member of the England team that won the World Cup. How did you do it, was there a secret?

JACK

No, we just had some good players. Sir Alf Ramsey said that England would win the World Cup before the World Cup took place. Everyone had a little smile.

BERNIE

Was he psychic?

JACK

We had people like Bobby Charlton, Bobby Moore and Jimmy Greaves, one of the top players in the business, and a lot of good players in the England squad, so it was no surprise when we won it really.

BERNIE

Do you think England will ever win it again?

JACK

Not the way we are going at the moment with so many foreign players. They seem to be taking the limelight rather than the English players, who are pushed into the background now. And our national team were never prepared properly for anything since that last World Cup. It's difficult to put your finger on why, but in every other country the national team is the pinnacle and the top. In England, you always get the impression that the league here is more important than anything else. The national side takes a second role to that. It's only in the last three or four years that they have actually allowed England players to cancel the game on the Saturday, so they have got time to prepare 10 days before an international match.

BERNIE

What kind of player were you? I've heard so many stories, I want to hear it from the horse's mouth?

JACK

I was awkward, a good competitor and I didn't like to lose. People have said I was uncompromising and I suppose they are right, I don't know.I couldn't play the way other people played. I was good at stopping other people playing, which people laugh at when you say it, but it's true.

I was a good keeper of the ball. I was a good tackler. I learned how to do things the right way in the North-east before I went away. Don't mess around in your 18-yard box, get rid of it, get it out, be effective.

I always believe that centre backs should be one-touch players. You don't want to be pulling balls down and doing clever things on the edge of your 18-yard box. If you make one mistake, you've lost the game.

Now in the English football league when they sign a centre back, they say he's great on the ball. That would frighten me to death. I don't like players who play centre back who are like that. I think you've got to be effective. I think in the years I played with Norman Hunter we were both effective.

BERNIE

You left Leeds after making over 600 league appearances and ended up joining Middlesbrough in the summer of 1973 as manager. How did that come about?

JACK

Doc Phillips was the England team doctor at that time and I had seen Middlesbrough play once before and thought they looked quite a good team.Stan Anderson was there at the time and they had some good players. I felt they just needed a couple of more players to make things happen. When I went, it was a team who had not quite done enough to get into the
Premier Division, or the First Division as it was called then.
Stan left and he had left me some good players. I mean, I found Graeme Souness playing left-back or left-half. He was never quick enough to play in those positions, so we moved him into

centre midfield. I had Alan Foggon, who was a winger, but I played him in midfield because he was a great runner and at that time the whole of the game was being played by teams who played strict offside. They would push up, so what you had to do was play the ball behind them and have somebody running from the midfield who wasn't offside. I tried to institute that at Middlesbrough when I went. The big problem with it was David Mills and John Hickton were both runners for the ball. John wanted to get to the far post and compete for headers and David Mills was quick at turning, but he was turning and running offside. So I introduced Alan Foggon into midfield alongside Graeme Souness. I got Bobby Murdoch and David Armstrong, who were both great passers of the ball, and we let Foggy run. When teams were pushing out to play offside, he would run from midfield and would play in behind them. The moment it got there we all backed it up and it worked a dream.

BERNIE

How did you manage to get Bobby Murdoch on a free from Celtic? Jock Stein must have been mad!

JACK

I don't know. I sat next to Jock at a football writers' dinner in London and he asked if I needed any help. I had just taken the Middlesbrough job and I said I was looking for a right-sided midfield player and one or two other players. He said he would give me Bobby Murdoch and I had to ask him if I'd heard him correctly. Give me Bobby Murdoch? He said not to worry about a fee, just look after Bobby.

BERNIE

You didn't get a bung did you Jack?

JACK

No, no. We looked after Bobby. When he arrived he was only 28 and was carrying a bit of weight. He worked very hard and became a great player for Middlesbrough for four years. He was one of the best passers of the ball you ever saw.

BERNIE

When you joined Boro you said you would last four years and you were true to your word. Why four years?

JACK

Well, I knew a big Labour man called Jim Bullock. He used to tell me never to stay in a job for longer than four years, because people get to anticipate you and they know exactly what you're thinking. You can't then start to introduce change because people won't accept it. The only way to introduce change is to find another club. So I did my four years, although I was tempted to stay another year because we had a few quid at Middlesbrough at that time.

BERNIE

Why didn't you spend the money?

JACK

I don't know. We had money and I could have bought and stayed another year and maybe we would have had a chance of winning something. But I decided that the four years was right, and that for any manager coming in behind me it wouldn't have been fair for me to spend the money that season, simply because he would want to spend it in his way. Whoever took my job took my place because it was my decision to leave, and I left. I once said to somebody doing an interview like this, probably the biggest mistake I made in management was not staying at Middlesbrough another year and I think that was probably right.

BERNIE

After leaving Middlesbrough you spent five years at Sheffield Wednesday before returning to the Boro as caretaker manager. Why caretaker?

JACK

Well, I did my five years at Sheff Wed and I was having a bit of time off. I've never gone from one club to another club to be manager, I've always had a little break in-between.
I was having my little break after Sheffield when Mike McCulloch phoned me up. Malcolm Allison had left and they were in a bit of trouble in the Second Division. He asked if I would come back and see them through the rest of the year. Considering Mike was a friend of mine - he joined the Middlesbrough board on the same day that I became manager - I said okay, but only until I've kept you in the division and we did, we stayed quite comfortably in the Division Then I left. Mike wanted me to stay but I didn't want to. That was me and I left.

BERNIE

On leaving the caretaker post you had a brief spell at Newcastle before being appointed Republic of Ireland manager. How did that come about?

JACK

Well, I never wanted the job at Newcastle, Jackie Milburn talked
me into it. He was on the phone to me all the time. They
couldn't find anybody to take the job funnily enough. Arthur
Cox had just left. They had got promotion, Kevin Keegan had
left, Terry McDermott was out of contract and looked like he
would be leaving and he did, and they asked me to keep them in
the First Division for a year. I agreed and we kept them in the
First Division and I got trapped in the job and couldn't find a
way out. I had to go to a tribunal with Chris Waddle at the end
of the season because he was going to Tottenham. Then when I
should have left I didn't and it finished up with the first excuse I
got, I was off. Paul Gascoigne was playing his first game in a
pre-season friendly against Sheffield United I think and a
section of the crowd started yelling 'Charlton out' at me. I
couldn't understand what it was for, because it was a pre-season
friendly and we hadn't even kicked a ball in the league yet. It
was apparently because I had being going to sign Eric Gates
from Ipswich, and he wanted too much and they wanted too
much and I cancelled the deal on the Friday. On the Saturday,
Lawrie McMenemie signed him for Sunderland, so really he had
become a Mackem rather than a Newcastle player and the crowd
didn't like that. It was my decision, but it gave me an excuse to
do what I wanted to do. I had done the year that I said I would
do and I wanted out but couldn't get out. It all finished up pretty
nasty. I really didn't want it to finish that way.

BERNIE

You went to the Republic after Newcastle. How did that come
about?

JACK

Well, I didn't go straight away. After I finished at Newcastle I wasn't doing anything. I got offered jobs in different places, then I was sat at home just before Christmas and got a phone call asking if I would be interested in the Irish job. I said I would be, then I went away to Spain for two or three weeks and when I got back I got another phone call to ask if I was still interested. I said I was, then I got another phone call to say I'd got the job, and that's when it all began. I just went away with the Irish and had a good look. I didn't know the first thing about the Irish and their football team or anything. I don't think anybody else did either. I got settled down to a way of playing, got the lads going a little bit and started to improve the team. The people in Ireland liked what I did and that's all that's really important.

BERNIE

Did you receive any stick from your mates, being English and joining the Republic?

JACK

No, not at all. I remember walking through Dublin on the day I got the job, and everyone in the streets just kept stopping me, shaking my hand and saying 'well done, hope you enjoy it, hope it works out for you'. I've always been well received by the people. I don't know why but the Irish took a liking to me. In fact, I'm probably one of the most popular Englishmen in Scotland funnily enough. For whatever reason they always love me when I go to Scotland, I don't know what it is.

BERNIE

As Republic boss you took Ireland to the European Championships in 1988 and two World Cup Finals in Italy and America. What was your greatest moment?

JACK

When you see the team improving and you're beating people, they are all good moments. I mean, we beat Brazil in Dublin and we beat any team in Europe that's of any consequence over the period that I was there. We did quite well in the World Cup in Italy and went to America and beat the Italians. We went down to Orlando and couldn't handle the heat but it was just one of those things. It finished not as well as we would have liked it to finish because I felt we had a good enough team to do well in America. But we didn't make it and I will always to this day blame the heat, because some of our players couldn't handle it at all. It was enjoyable with the Irish. The games you get the most pleasure from are the ones you win that qualify you for the big competitions. And strangely enough we never qualified in Dublin, we always qualified away from home for various competitions.

BERNIE

Every time you called up a player to the national squad people questioned their background. Did that annoy you?

JACK

It did and it still does to this day. The qualification for Ireland is exactly the same as for England, Northern Ireland, Scotland and Wales. You can go back as far as your grandmother to qualify to play for that country if you can prove her place of origin to be in that country. That happened when I brought in John Aldridge and Ray Houghton. Ray Houghton was born in Glasgow and he's a Glaswegian, but his father was born in Donegal, so he's well qualified to play for the Republic. John Aldridge on the other hand, we had a hell of a job finding where the church was that his grandmother was married and buried in. When we found it he could get a passport and qualify. People made a big deal of this but, I mean, Ireland was only a small country and we didn't have any number of players playing. We had to get players from where we could. If they qualified, we had to get them. I couldn't pick a team out of the league in Ireland - that wouldn't qualify for anything. If you want to compete with the best in the World Cup you have to get the best players you can, which is what I did.

We had a good nucleus of solid Irish people - Kevin Moran, Mick McCarthy, Paul McGrath, Tony Galvin. I mean, the ones that had been questioned were actually before me. Mark Lawrenson was questionable, but Mark was great for us up until he got injured. I did get annoyed and I'm answering the question in a long way this time because it still annoys me. The complaints come from people who couldn't beat us, like the English. They couldn't beat us and they didn't like it.

BERNIE

You left the Republic job in the 1994/95 season. Was the timing right?

JACK

I was always going to retire. Like I mentioned earlier, Jimmy Bullock also advised me to retire at 50 if I could afford to.

BERNIE

You could certainly afford it Jack!

JACK

Not when I was 50 I couldn't. If you can afford to retire when you're 50, do so, because you then go into the last 10 years or so of your life fit enough and able enough to do the things that you want to do, not the things you've had to do. I never made it at 50 but I made it at 60. I resigned and virtually told them on my 60th birthday that I would be leaving at the end of the qualification. If we qualified, I would stay over the summer. If we didn't qualify, I would leave the day we didn't, and they knew that from the day I turned 60. We had a party in Bolton, everybody came over. I was always going to retire at 60 and I did.

BERNIE

Why have you never managed England? Would you like to have managed England?

JACK

Everybody that played for their country would like to manage their country one day. I felt I was overlooked by the English. Strangely enough, I was a staff coach with the FA from a very early age and I had always been an FA lad. I had always done my badges, all the coaching certificates and all the things that were necessary. I had played for England, I had played for teams that had played all over Europe, my qualifications were not in question. Maybe it was just me, my personality. Maybe they didn't want someone like me in that sort of situation? I mean, Brian Clough never got the job either. I remember two or three members of the committee that were picking the team phoned

me and asked me to apply, so I did. I never got a reply to the letter but they had people there who had nowhere
near my qualifications or played at the levels that I had played at, or looked at the levels that I had looked at. I worked for ITV for years, I was at every game that was important anywhere in Europe. I was at every World Cup, I knew international football inside out, but I never got an invitation to manage the England team. I would have liked to have been asked but I never was.

BERNIE

Well Jack, thanks very much for talking to me. I love that jumper you're wearing by the way!

JACK (With a massive grin) Okay Bernie, let's go fishing

HONOURS

JACK CHARLTON

PLAYING CAREER HISTORY

1952-1973 Leeds United
1965-1970 England.

MANAGING CAREER HISTORY

1973-1977 Middlesbrough
1977-1983 Sheffield Wed
1984   Middlesbrough (caretaker)
1984-1985 Newcastle United
1986-1994 Republic of Ireland.

PLAYING HONOURS (winners)

Leeds
1969 Football League Champions
1964 Division 2 Champions
1972 FA Cup
1968 League Cup
1968 Inter Cities Fairs Cup

England
1966 World Cup

MANAGERIAL HONOURS (winners)

Sheffield Wed
1980 Division 3 Promotion

Middlesbrough
1974   Manager of The Year
1973-1974 Football League 2nd division

CAPS 35 Full caps for England.

JACK CHARLTON OBE

Jack joins in the celebrations, World Cup 1966

Typical Charlton pose while at Leeds United.

"The nearest anybody came was Gary Lineker over in Spain and I will never forget it - it was in the 1980s. I was wallpapering my dining room and I was listening to the Spain against England game and he got to four. I was thinking he couldn't equal my record over in Spain."

Referring to lineker almost equalling his 5 goals against cyprus.

MALCOLM MACDONALD
NEWCASTLE

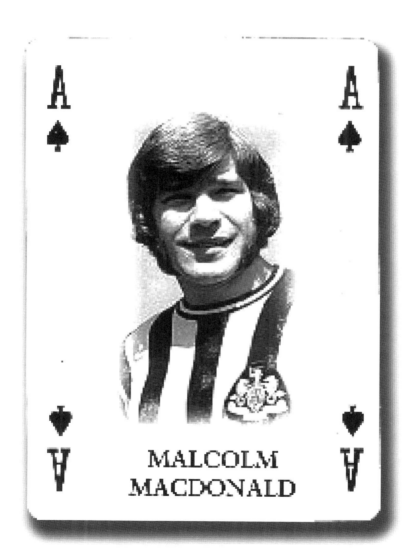

MALCOLM
MACDONALD

Malcolm Ian Macdonald was born on January 7, 1950.
He signed for Newcastle in 1971 and made his debut against
Liverpool,scoring a terrific hat-trick and living up to his
nickname Supermac. Malcolm was lightning quick, super
strong, direct and had a one-track mind to score goals.

I first heard of Malcolm when I was a kid in Glasgow, despite
not knowing who he was. If you had side burns, your mates
would say: "They are some pair of Supermacs!"
When I arrived in England, I'd seen Malcolm at stadiums up and
down the country over the years without making contact.

Our first meeting was when we linked up to do the Three
Legends show at Century Radio.
I find Malcolm smart, articulate and headstrong.
On the show I look at him as the headmaster and myself and
Micky Horswill as the pupils. For me, that's the perfect
ingredient.

I didn't have to travel far to meet up with Malcolm - I
interviewed him in the Real Radio studio at Team Valley.
Once he started talking, I couldn't shut him up!

BERNIE

You were born in Fulham, London. Was your upbringing a posh
one?

MALCOLM

No, not really (laughs). Although I have to say, where we lived
was a nice area - Finlay Street. It led up to Fulham football
ground and Bishops Park ran from one end of the football park
up to Putney Bridge.

Off that came the Bishop of London's residence, with tennis courts coming off that, and opposite them were very nice flats. It was a very, very large semi which I lived in and when I was first born,basically there was three parts of my mother's family in there. We were one third of it as it were. There was our eldest sister on the ground floor, we were upstairs, and upstairs again was another aunt and then the ground floor aunt left for the south coast so my mother had a few more children after me. I had three younger brothers and we sort of spread out downwards into the house, so there was plenty of space. Bishops Park was up the road and that was all I needed. All the kids would meet up there and play football in the school holidays. It would be four jumpers down on the ground and we used to play football from eight in the morning until eight at night and that was all I ever did(laughs).

BERNIE

You began your career at non-league Tonbridge. Was that a good grooming before turning professional?

MALCOLM

Yes, it was a very good grooming, more from the people who were in it than the club itself. But then I suppose football clubs are all about the personalities who are there. Tonbridge and Tunbridge Wells are easily confused. But this was Tunbridge, which is a very old historical town that goes back absolute centuries. There's a famous upper class school there and where we used to play was one of Kent's old county cricket grounds and it had been turned into a football stadium. So if you can imagine the size of a big round arena - they built a stand around one side, then there was a football pitch and then they built terraces. Behind the terraces there was still a huge area and that's where we used to train. It was absolutely brilliant, we used to change in the cricket pavilion.

BERNIE

How old were you while you were at Tonbridge?

MALCOLM

I went there when I was 17. I'd been at Barnet before when I was at school in London and they wanted to play me but the headmaster at the school refused to allow me to play for them.

BERNIE

Why was that?

MALCOLM

His reasoning was that I had to do better in school work, and school work was everything. He stopped me playing for Barnet and his reasoning was to get me focused and concentrating on lessons. My father said he wasn't having it, so he marched along to the school to see the headmaster.

The headmaster was a New Zealander who preferred rugby, despite it being a football school. It was a small grammar school which had prided itself on two things, one being its Shakespearean plays. A rugby man at a footballing school didn't go down too well and he didn't see the importance of football and my father went to see him just to have the conversation of parent and headmaster.

My father was a very good-humoured Yorkshireman and after the meeting he said: "I've never met such an ignorant, bombastic arsehole in my life." He said: "Son, if you want to leave school and follow your feelings and have the career that you want, I will back you 100%."

I was just coming up to 16 and I said: "Yes, I want to become a professional footballer." My father wasn't very well at the time. He had a coronary thrombosis and had a couple of heart attacks, so he was not in the best of health. He was struggling, but nevertheless he found the strength and the time to take part with me in all of this and he backed me. After my father's blessing to go and become a professional footballer, I just went for it.

BERNIE

You signed for Fulham when you were 19?

MALCOLM

(Laughs) Prior to all the nonsense, which happened at the grammar school, I found myself, like most professional footballers I think, sort of thrown forward in ages. So when I was seven or eight I found myself playing with the 11-year-olds. When I got to grammar school aged 12, very quickly I was playing with the 14 and 15-year-olds. And by the time I was 14 I was playing with the 18-year-olds. So I was 15 just turned and the sports teacher told me he was going to put me in the London Grammar Schools' football trials. He asked what position I wanted to be put down as. When I played my own age I played centre half, centre midfield or centre forward. The better players tended to play through the middle. When I played for the schools first team I would play usually outside left. Most of the lads in the trials were going to be 18 or 19 and I was a rather diminutive 15-year-old. I thought there were two positions where size doesn't matter, either on the wing or at left-back, so I said to put me in at left-back because left footers are valued. I got in the London Grammar School team and I was spotted by one of the coaches there, a fellow called Terry Casey who played for Barnet and England amateurs. I did okay for the grammar side and I was also invited along to Barnet - that's when the problems started with the headmaster. He stopped me continuing with Barnet. I left there but having left school some while later, my father was getting much more ill and so he couldn't continue. He was a painter and decorator by trade. So we decided to move and the way for him to move forward was if we bought a confectionery and tobacconist shop that he could run. So the house was put on the market. They now sell for about £1.5 million in Fulham - he sold it for £6,750 in 1966. We agreed the sale about three weeks before Christmas and sadly he died on that Christmas Day. My mother had four sons and I was 16, just about to turn 17, and so I sort of became the head of the household. A lot of responsibility was thrown on my shoulders because we were committed to the move. So I had to organise not just the house move - because my mother was grieving desperately - but also I had to oversee the buying of the business and taking the business over as well.I'd been pretty active in all sorts of things in earning money while in London, so I had a bit of experience - more than most kids would get. So I went down there and I was running the shop really for my mother.

She was looking after the kids, all of them were still at school, so we tried to keep things all going and we were a bit isolated down in Sussex. I was desperate to start playing football again - I'd gone six months without playing. It was just concentrating on getting the business running and so I started taking driving lessons. I got talking with the driving instructor and told him I was desperate to play football again but I'd looked at the football in Sussex and I wasn't all that impressed by the level of it. He said there was a terrific side over in Kent called Knowle Juniors run by a fellow called George Piper. So I went and played over there. I'd played three games for them and the next thing Harry Haslam was knocking on my door. Harry Haslam had been at Manchester United and he was now the manager at

Tonbridge, but he had played for many years at Manchester United. He signed me for Tonbridge football club as a part-time professional and I was on eight quid a week - I felt like I had won the pools.

It was really good money - £1 a draw, £2 a win, and we were playing three games a week sometimes.I could win £6 in bonuses because we weren't a bad side. Plus, I was getting expenses for all the petrol going from Forest Row in Sussex to Tonbridge. I could be taking home 20 quid, it was unbelievable, plus I was working in the shop. I have to say I learnt a lot of great lessons in life from Harry. Invariably, I could be late after working in the shop. One time after training the fellow came round handing out the pay packets and there was a really big, heavy one. Harry came across and told the club secretary he would give it to me. When I opened it up it was a tenner light and there was a wrist watch in it.

He said: "You won't be bloody late again will you son?"

It was the greatest lesson I learned - don't be late. It cost me a tenner and I had a wrist watch for it. He could have screamed and shouted but he always found a better way to get the message home.

BERNIE

What about your stint at Fulham?

MALCOLM

It wasn't too difficult, except I had so much to learn about the game, I really did. I was a quick learner but I had heaps to learn. Bobby Robson had taken over after two spells there as a player and Fulham was my club.

I'd been a supporter since the age of four and saw my first game at Craven Cottage against Blackburn. I fell in love with football, the crunch of the studs in the turf and the even greater crunch in the tackling, and Fulham was exactly where I wanted to be. I could have signed for Crystal Palace but my heart took me to Fulham. As I said, Bobby Robson was the manager and the first lesson I learned was never seek to manage your old teammates - it really doesn't work. And it didn't work for Bobby Robson, bless him. They were very difficult times.He had lost a whole load of players through injury and he put me up front in the late October, early November of the season. I had been playing up front because of injuries in the reserves and scored a few goals. So he put me in the first team and I played up front with a fellow called Frank Large. He was a big blond lad who was awkward and brave as a lion. He knocked people all over the place and things would bounce off him. I just used my pace and I played six games and scored five goals.

Bobby Robson was sacked and I was dropped even though I was the club's top goal scorer. I remained the top scorer until two games from the end of the season and the club got relegated. This was my club that I loved always as a kid and my hero was Johnny Haynes. What a passer of the ball. He was an absolutely wonderful player. To this day I still don't know if he was right-footed or left-footed - he was so two-footed it was untrue.

All of a sudden I was playing with him and it really was incredible. But my hero became almost like my enemy and not through any fault of my own.

Bobby Robson left, Johnny Haynes became caretaker manager and dropped me.

BERNIE

So your boyhood hero turned into a villain?

MALCOLM

Yes, he really did. I was so upset about it all as well so I just went into the reserves. I just kept scoring goals and I kept learning as much as possible, although there wasn't much help coming from people. Everybody was fighting their own corner as it were. It was a club that had been relegated from just before I had arrived and got relegated the season before from the First Division for the first time in three decades or something like that, and the whole thing was very fraught. When you're a 28-year-old lad all you want is a bit of stability and a steady platform. Just to learn and not be constantly pilloried and away from all that which was going on. It became quite a depressing place to be. At the end of the season I went to see Tommy Trinder, who was a great comedian and the club chairman. I told him I couldn't stay there, I had to go, but he told me I was staying.

I said, for one, I couldn't afford it. I had signed for £20 a week and it was no good to me. It was okay when I was part time at Tonbridge, I was laughing. But I was having to travel 70 miles a day.

BERNIE

You ended up going to Luton for £17,500.

MALCOLM

Yes, Alec Stock came in and bought me.

BERNIE

Did it come as a surprise?

MALCOLM

No, I knew it was going to happen. They paid a lot of money for me, 17½ grand. I suppose I'd played about 12 games but really I had that spell playing six games and scored five goals. I learned the greatest lesson in my life from this man Alec Stock, to focus on what is and what isn't important.

I hadn't been with Alec Stock any more than six months and I realised I had worked out life for an individual. I sat down and I worked out what my strengths were. I was prepared to accept every individual has a million weaknesses and I'm exactly the same. But I didn't give a stuff, I only focused on what I was good at, what my strengths were, just go that way and don't worry about anything else. That's how I went through football, just playing to my strengths and looking to play to other people's strengths.

Alec Stock gave me the greatest shock of my life the day before the first game. He came into the dressing room and he said he hoped we were going to get promotion and he asked us our thoughts. He said he was going to tell us how to do it and he made it sound so simple. He said we had 46 games to play, could only afford to lose nine and the wins and draws would look after themselves. To do that we had to let in no more than 36 goals and score 82 or more, simple as that.

And he just went round giving everybody a target.

He said: "Macdonald, the new boy - 30!"

BERNIE

How did you feel?

MALCOLM

I wasn't exactly bricking it but I was dumbstruck. I really was. I actually nudged the experienced Welsh centre forward next to me and asked if I'd heard right. He said: "You heard him right boy and f*****g good luck to you." I needed it!

BERNIE

As the season rolled on did you achieve it?

MALCOLM

I was one short - I got 29 and we got promotion. Leyton Orient were champions and we were second. I went across to Alex Stock with two glasses of champagne and I gave him a glass and I held the other one up and said: "Well boss, here's to playing in the Second Division next season." And I said: "I've got an apology to make. I missed your target of 30, I only got 29." He told me I'd had a bloody good go at it and I'd enjoy playing at a much better level next season - and that I owed him one! (Laughs) Here I was sipping champagne and he had already set me a target for the following season - 31. So he did exactly the same in the team meeting prior to the first game but it didn't matter, because I knew what he was going to say. At about Easter time we blew it, so promotion flew out of the window and we got to the last game of the season and I was on 29. We had to beat Cardiff in our last game of the season by two clear goals to go into the Watney Cup instead of Cardiff. So it was a better Cup Final because the Watney Cup was big time stuff for the lower divisions. I finished up scoring three. I knew it was my last game for Luton so it was great to go out in a blaze of glory, scoring a hat-trick, winning 3-0 and going into the Watney Cup. I walked into the dressing room and I'd got 32 goals. I said to Alec Stock: "Well, there you go boss, there's the one that I owe you and one for luck." He said: "You'll f*****g need it where you're going old son!" (Laughs) It was then that he told me that there were clubs in for me and as they hadn't got promotion that I'd be on my way in the summer.

BERNIE

After two years at the Hatters, scoring 49 goals in 88 league games, you signed for Newcastle. What was the attraction of Newcastle?

MALCOLM

Well, they had just won the Fairs Cup, remember?
A couple of years before they had won a European competition and that made them a rarity. Plus the fact that dear old Harry Haslam, who had been my manager at Tonbridge, had been Bobby Robson's chief scout then gone on to Luton. He was the chief scout in my two years at Luton and he was a mentor for me. He pulled me to one side and he said: "They will love you up there, they love their centre forwards."
I didn't really know much about the North East to be honest.
I had never played at Newcastle but he gave me the lowdown on what it was about and he talked to Jackie Milburn and Hughie Gallagher. He told me that if I scored goals up there I would be loved for ever more and how right he was. There was talk of Manchester United and there was talk of Chelsea. I didn't fancy Chelsea much because I was a Fulham lad and a Fulham supporter. No matter the falling out I'd had, Chelsea were the enemy. You would never have signed for Rangers, Bernie.

BERNIE

No way.

MALCOLM

Could you imagine you in a blue shirt?

BERNIE

No I couldn't ever see myself in a blue shirt.

MALCOLM

So I signed and arrived in the North East, did the press conference and a chap came across to me. He was casually but smartly dressed, and warmly shook my hand. He said: "I wish you so much luck. Do well here at Newcastle and they will love you. Just keep shooting. By the way, my name's Jackie Milburn." The great Jackie Milburn, of course I had heard of him, and straight away before I had the chance to get a word out he said: "You'll be looking for a house fairly soon, you want to get yourself up and settled before the season starts." I met Jackie at 10am on the Friday at St James's Park after I'd been home and he took me on a tour in his car and taught me a fantastic lesson. He let me know what the North East was all about and he took me all down the coast and pointed out the pit where he worked. He told me how he could play football the same as me, run like the wind and stick the ball in the net and he was given the chance to play professionally. All of these years later his schoolmates and friends who he left down the pit were still down there, working underground and finishing up as black as coal. He said: "Remember this. On a Friday, those guys come out and clean the whole week's grime off their bodies.
"They have a couple of pints and then the next day, they get the bus from Ashington to St James's Park in Newcastle.
"And at 2pm they will be there on the terraces screaming and cheering for their team, Newcastle United.
"At 3pm they will have been cheering for an hour and you now start." He said: "You've now got an hour an a half, because from Monday to Friday they have been working in pitch black, no oxygen, in the most terrible circumstances."He said: "This is

155

their moment of relief and enjoyment, their entertainment and amusement, and they have come to watch you.

"The least you can do for an hour and a half every time you get the ball is attack the centre half, beat every man that's in front of you, rain shots on goal and stick as many balls in the net as you can. "And when you're not scoring, be as near to scoring as you can and create the excitement on the terraces they need, a little relief from working down the pit five days a week." He said: "There you go, easy as that." And it worked because he gave me a little insight into the mentality. Someone else once said to me if it wasn't Jackie it might have been Joe Harvey. He said: "Up here they have three loves and they come in a very specific order.

"The beer, the football, the women - they come in that order. "It has never changed so you always know how to make them happy, simple as that. "Give them a beer, play some good football and then they can go home to their wives."

BERNIE

You arrived at Newcastle in a Rolls Royce. Was that a statement, an arrogance, a publicity stunt?

MALCOLM

(Laughs) It was more Luton Town Football Club and Alex Stock saying: "Go up there in style old son and let them know you have arrived!" That's what he told me to do and he got one of the sponsors of the club - a car driver - to loan me a Rolls Royce. One of the company directors drove me up and when we were crossing the Tyne Bridge he put a chauffeur's hat on. So I was chauffeur-driven into St James's Park and the Rolls Royce pulled in front of the steps that led up to the main entrance and it was full. There was a gaggle of press there with microphones and cameras and televisions, notebooks and pencils and all sorts. So the director of the car company got out, walked around and opened the back door for me to step out. And as I'm stepping out a voice right in the middle of the gaggle of press guys said in a sort of stage whisper: "That's the first time I've actually seen a player arrive in his signing-on fee!" (Laughs) That was my first brush with Geordie humour and it's a great humour as well.

BERNIE

When you signed, were you aware of the tradition of the Number 9 shirt?

MALCOLM

Not fully, no. When I signed I wasn't fully aware of it. But I very quickly became aware of it - people were on at me all the time. You could imagine centre forwards arriving at Newcastle and becoming overwhelmed by the pressure that they are put under. With me though, scoring goals is all I wanted to do. I was just there to score goals.
Alex Stock had thrown me a target of 30 goals for the previous two seasons, so I had been playing under that pressure. At the press conference at St James's Park I was asked if I had a target for my first season, and I said it was to score 30 goals. The headline in about four papers the next day was 'Supermouth'. They just thought I was a bragger.

BERNIE

But you were being honest, weren't you?

MALCOLM

I was being honest and if they had looked at my record carefully they would have seen that I had played two seasons for Luton Town and scored 61 goals. So that certainly was my target. In my first season at Newcastle I was about three short. It wasn't the best of teams.

BERNIE

What was your philosophy as a striker?

MALCOLM

My philosophy, quite frankly, was that it was down to everybody else to stop us from losing games, it was down to me to win them.

BERNIE

How good was your partnership with John Tudor?

MALCOLM

We were totally different, but we complemented each other. Opposites attract and John was a great theoriser and thinker. He would come up with all sorts and I suppose I upset the equilibrium to a degree to start with, because I got it, turned and I ran for goal and had a shot (laughs). John would say: "No, no, think about it" and I said: "I did think about it John, I thought about it two years ago." My thoughts were get it, turn and shoot - simple as that. And if you can do it as quickly as you can say it you've got a chance of being a successful, top quality goal scorer. Harry Haslam, used to actually get me doing that in practice. I used to go into an empty Co-Op warehouse with a plastic Johnny Giles Ball. It was the only time I got near enough to kick Johnny Giles, he was a crafty so and so! And literally I would shoot against a wall, then I had to get it, control it and turn and shoot against the other wall.

Get it, turn and shoot, that's all I did and I used to do that four afternoons a week until I collapsed through exhaustion, hunger and dizziness from all of the constant turning and spinning. Other footballers didn't understand that philosophy. Passing was only ever the second option for me. Terry Hibbert understood it perfectly. He knew exactly what I was about. He just said: "When it's on, I'll knock you in."

BERNIE

You moved to Arsenal and the goals continued to flow up until 1979, when injury forced your premature retirement at the age of 29. What was the injury and how did you cope?

MALCOLM

It started off with a cartilage operation. After the plaster came off two weeks after the operation, I couldn't straighten my legs at all. Weeks went by, I was doing all the remedials but I couldn't actually straighten it. If you don't fully straighten it then you don't fully recover all the muscle on the thigh. They sent me to a specialist in Harley Street. He was the only man who had this particular X-ray machine called an arthrogram. He must have taken about 150 pictures and when he looked at all of them he couldn't find anything in the joint. Then he looked at one and went: "Ah, now, there's a tiny little speck there." It was so tiny you could hardly see it, but based on that and the problems I'd had he advised that they open me up and they did. What they found was the very end of it was pencil lead thickness and it turned out to be over 14 inches long. It sort of

159

zig-zagged its way through the knee joint and it all went back to me having a knee operation and my cartilage removed when I was playing for Newcastle back in 1973.

The surgeon had left the attachment and the cartilage. It's attached at both ends, the blood flows in at one end and goes out at the other. Where he had taken the torn cartilage out, he had left the attachment where the blood flowed and it seemed the medical profession thought at that time,if they left that attachment that possibly a new cartilage would grow. It was a bit of a risk to take as a professional footballer. It wasn't the cartilage that grew, it was this gristle type thing that went all the way through wherever it could find a space in the knee joint and it caused me untold problems,

plus a huge amount of damage to the knee joint.

They opened it and removed it. This meant that I had the knee opened three times, and basically they say you can get away with two but the third time, that's it, you never recover.

BERNIE

So how did you cope?

MALCOLM

Well, I worked hard for months and months and months in an effort to get fit. I was just getting back to full fitness as Arsenal were due to play at Wembley in the FA Cup final against Manchester United. Terry Neill, the manager of Arsenal, was tossing up whether or not I should play and in the end he went for Frank Stapleton and Alan Sunderland.

As it so happens it worked out because Alan Sunderland scored in the dying seconds and won the game. But I was sort of 13th man - of course there was only the one substitute then. Then there was the final league match of the season, on the following Tuesday night, at Stamford Bridge.

I played and scored and we drew 1-1. Having been out for a number of months, the one thing I needed was games. I needed to get myself fit. So I got it organised to go and play over in Sweden for Djurgarden. I lasted 80 minutes in the first game and my knee started to really hurt.

It was 70 minutes in the second game, 60 minutes in the third. It was getting 10 minutes less every game I played. The last one I played in I got about 20 minutes and I couldn't continue. I knew I was on my last legs.

I went back to Arsenal. Don Howe created this 12 minute run where you just have to run as far as you can around a lap track. He was the first person to introduce that into football. So I did it and got to about eight minutes and that was it, the knee just wouldn't take my weight again.

So I said: "Look, I've had it" and they talked to me about becoming a David Fairclough on the bench, just to go on and be an impact player, a bit like kickers in American football.

But I said that wasn't for me. So Arsenal were very good, although I felt very guilty because they had paid a lot of money for me and they had only had two full seasons out of me.I always like to give people their money's worth, but it was one of those things and Arsenal didn't insure their players. But I had a super time there, it was a wonderful club Arsenal, it really was. It's a very special place and they always make me welcome. To this very day they will phone me up. It doesn't matter how many times you move, they always seem to find your number.

They always keep me involved, it's nice what Arsenal do. They do tours of the stadium and they employ ex-players to do that. I look at other clubs which I've been involved with and ex-players would be the last people they would want involved. They always make you welcome.

BERNIE

What do you make of modern day players' wages, in comparison with wages in your days? Any resentment towards it?

MALCOLM

None whatsoever, because I actually was an advocate for freedom of contract. Contracts never used to put you in a position where you could determine your own future.
So I actually took legal advice. I wrote to Newcastle United and they more or less weren't even prepared to discuss the matter. I wanted just to discuss it and they didn't want to know. It wasn't long after I retired that the form of the contract changed and freedom of contract came in.
So once your contract ended, you were then free to make the decision as to what you wanted to do, whether you wanted to stay or move on. You got paid according to your status, not just because you were tied. I think Graham Rix of Arsenal was one of the first to benefit by that kind of contract.
I don't begrudge players getting what they do, as long as they go and earn it and that is the key issue. It's not whether they're being overpaid, it's whether they go out and truly earn the money. I feel that footballers in the 1970s were perhaps putting more into the game for a mere pittance compared to what the players get now. People must remember that footballers are young, they're very young. If you're not young you can't play the game - you have to be young to play it. They haven't got maturity, haven't got experience and they are learning all the time about everything - not just football, about life, business and all sorts. They have to learn their lessons as they go along. I feel that perhaps they don't understand the gravity of signing a contract and what they really mean and the expectations of the

people at the football club, and that includes the supporters of course.
I think there are far too many players in professional football nowadays who you could ask if they are repaying their contract.

BERNIE

You made 14 appearances for England. Should it have been more?

MALCOLM

If Alf Ramsey had remained as manager it probably would have been more. That was the most dreadful thing that the Football Association did, sack Alf Ramsey. He was the only man who had ever won the World Cup for England. He was in a phase where he was starting to move out the 1966 winners.
Now that was a very difficult task. He couldn't do it en masse, so he was steadily doing it and bringing in players.
I remember going to Portugal and Alf Ramsey said: "The FA have come to me and said that I'm unfriendly towards the press. "Well of course I am," he said, "because they are not going to do us any favours are they?
"But the request has been made that the press be allowed to have a whole afternoon, with all of you players in a conference room and they can speak to you individually."
He said: "Now I've got to give an answer on this, so I'm asking you. So what would you like to do?"
So we spoke amongst ourselves and said we didn't fancy it and he went back and said he, rather than the players, had decided against it. We played against Portugal and drew 0-0, and the team was a completely new one. The only old face in it was Alan Ball. There was Keegan, Brooking, Shannon, myself, Dave Thomas and a host of others. All the young 20-somethings in the game were all there in the England squad.

If you remember, Alan Ball won a World Cup medal at 19, so he hadn't reached 30. So we went out and drew 0-0 with Portugal - we absolutely murdered them and missed so many goals it was untrue.

If we had beaten them 6-1 it may have been a fair reflection on the game.

The football we played was absolutely brilliant, it really was. It was wonderful to be part of that game. It was disappointing that we hadn't won but the football was scintillating. We expected to see headlines the next day about this being the start of the new England. But they absolutely pilloried Ramsey, slaughtered him and chopped his legs away from him. It was evil what they did. The FA sacked him and that was his last game. It was a fabulous England team.

We all knew that if we just got the first there would be another five to follow and we were just brimming with confidence after the game. He was rubbing his hands and thanking us for a wonderful performance and said: "This is just the start of something that's going to be very, very big." He was full of enthusiasm.

But the FA sacked him and we had drawn 0-0 over in Portugal, in Lisbon. There had been a huge partisan crowd at the Stadium of Light and they were baying for our blood. But we murdered them, we embarrassed them but just couldn't score and we were horrified.

BERNIE

So when Alf went was that your chances limited internationally?

MALCOLM

Yes. Joe Mercer came in as caretaker and he wanted to do his own thing. Then he was followed by a full time manager - Don Revie. I wasn't a Revie-type player and he left me out after three games. They were struggling for goals and there was a big press clamour, loads of headlines, to get me into the side. I came in and played against West Germany and scored in a 2-0 win against a side which included Franz Beckenbauer at centre half and Berti Vogts at left-back.

We absolutely hammered them and in the next game I scored five goals against Cyprus. So I'd played two games and scored six goals and Revie just couldn't wait to get rid of me. My goals sort of saved Revie to a degree and he couldn't get rid of me quick enough.

BERNIE

Talking about five against Cyprus, which has been well documented, are you amazed that all these years later no player has ever beaten it?

MALCOLM

No, I'm not to be honest. The nearest anybody came was Gary Lineker over in Spain and I will never forget it - it was in the 1980s. I was wallpapering my dining room and I was listening to the Spain against England game and he got to four. I was thinking he couldn't equal my record over in Spain, and as it happened he didn't. That was the nearest anybody really came to it and I'm not surprised it has never been beaten because five goals takes some doing. Plus the fact there aren't many as greedy as me! You know what I'm talking about. It's that attitude of mind. Lineker certainly had it but there's not been many since. There's nobody in the game with that kind of attitude now I don't think.

BERNIE

Do you reckon that record will stand for years to come?

165

MALCOLM

Probably, yeah. I would think so.

BERNIE

What were your qualities as a player?

MALCOLM

I was lightning quick, I was hugely strong. In the factsheets that they all used to do, for some reason they always had me down as 5ft 8in and 11 stone.

BERNIE

Was that with or without your high heels? (Laughs)

MALCOLM

The truth of the matter was that I was 5ft 10 and a half and 13 and a half stone. If anybody came in and hit me they bounced off, basically. I had a very low centre of gravity and so my balance was spot on and very powerful. So once I started shifting, nobody was going to take me down. It needed a really huge effort - strength and pace. I had a huge leap as well, so I got a lot of headed goals. If you look at the goals that I scored, a third were with my left foot, a third with my head and a third with my right foot. That's how it worked.

What I did was I worked a lot on my right foot because as a left footed player facing a centre half, in the main they were always going to be right footed. So if I went onto my left foot, I went onto my strong foot, so I always looked to go on my right. I perfected a good shot with it and worked hard at getting up in the air and attacking the far post.

BERNIE

What do you think you lacked as a player? If anything.

MALCOLM

Stamina. I was a sprinter. Long distance was never, ever for me. I could do 100 metres in 10.4 seconds, so I was never going to be a long distance runner. But I could go in short bursts and keep going for a very long time on that. I watch forwards now and I see them looking to link up and I never did that. I would do it begrudgingly, when it was absolutely necessary. But all the time I was thinking how I could score a goal. Harry Haslam said at Luton that you should score once in every six touches and that's how I remembered it. Maybe what he said to me was you should have a shot once in every six touches. But the way I remember it, for every six touches I had to get a shot in, so I just literally thought about getting a shot in. I didn't think passing, it didn't make me greedy so much but it made me very tunnel visioned towards the opposing goal. How can I get from here to there as quickly as possible in the straightest of lines?
It's a way of thinking that midfield players will never understand.
Defenders certainly will never understand and yet they had to play against me. That's how they couldn't handle me. They couldn't even begin to get onto my wavelength. Yours was quite similar. You're one of the rare people on this planet that really understands what I'm talking about.

BERNIE

I know exactly what you're talking about.

MALCOLM

But most people finish off by saying you're a greedy bastard. You have 10 people to defend the goal, you have one to attack the other and I was that one.

BERNIE

You became manager of Fulham. Was that something you always fancied?

MALCOLM

No, it wasn't. I didn't fancy it at all. I'd never fancied management while I'd been a player and I thought it was a thankless job. I retired at 29 and I'd never fully satisfied all the desires inside and an opportunity came along.
It was like looking a gift horse in the mouth and then turning away from it if I said no. So I thought about it long and hard and I thought I'd never forgive myself if I didn't have a go. So I took over Fulham after Bobby Campbell was the manager. He had been a very strict disciplinarian and I went in there and there was literally fear in the dressing room.
People were jumpy, they were nervous and so nobody was themselves in any way to play football, when you need to relax. You need to feel confident and nobody was like that at all. I went in there and brought in a regime of piss-taking and got everybody laughing. All of a sudden I was the butt of a lot of the piss-taking, but that was fine, it didn't matter, it just got everybody in it together. Even to the point where on a Friday, when I felt that people were a bit tense I'd tell everybody to meet in the bar at 7pm and I'd buy them all a pint of beer. We would go and have a meal and the senior players could have another pint afterwards, but that was it, nobody left the hotel. I think people became aware of each other more because of that

168

and they went out on a Saturday fighting and scrapping together.

BERNIE

Bruce Rioch did similar things to that. After your stint at Craven Cottage, you quit the game and became a landlord. Why a landlord?

MALCOLM

My marriage had broken up and I have to say, there was all sorts of things going on at Fulham FC. I was the manager and the chairman played a two-faced game on me. He was making out that he was all in support, but in actual fact he really did pull the rug from underneath me. It was all very unnecessary what he did. In the end he caused a lot of people a lot of heartache. I resigned from Fulham and and there was talk of Terry Venables - who was at QPR at the time - going to Barcelona. My marriage was on the rocks and when he went all of the attention was then suddenly turned on me, almost as if someone had told them. In fact, I had an idea who contacted the press. It's not the sports guys you deal with in situations like that, all of a sudden you get the news hounds on you. It wasn't very pleasant and it made for a very, very difficult period. I had a chat with Ray Harford, who was my coach at Fulham, after I'd left and he said he was sorry to see what happened. He said he hoped I didn't feel that he had to gain from it and I said it was no problem and he should just get on and do the job, that's life. He told me that past history usually says I would be back in the game in 12 months. He was wrong. It took me three years before I ever had a sniff of anything in the game. I joined Huddersfield for a brief spell. They had been down in the doldrums for about five years, just fighting off relegation.
They had got a new owner and a new chairman. I had known the fellow for some years and he contacted me and invited me up

for a chat because he was looking for a new manager. So I went up there and said: "Look, I'll tell you now. The word in the game is that you, this club, have got yourselves into such a hole that anybody would be a fool to take the job, to be honest."
He said: "I know that it's a hell of a task, there's going to be a lot of pitfalls before it can be turned around I know that we are facing relegation. "We are not going to ask you to stave off relegation, if we get relegated, that's fine."
And so this was the conversation in the October.
He said: "Let's just build the club on a long-term basis if it's a job that's going to take four or five years." I thought: "Blimey!"

BERNIE

How long did it last?

MALCOLM

So I agreed. I sold my business and I went wholeheartedly into it. Just after Christmas he told me he was having to move to the Isle of Man for tax reasons and so he was leaving the football club. All of a sudden the five year plan wasn't even going to make five months. I'd sold my business and I was left up the river without a paddle and then
lost my canoe, because the old chairman got back in.
I'd given him some terrible stick as manager of Fulham. He was one of the real old school, and I mean First World War.
Football had moved on, but I congratulated him on getting back in and asked when he would like me to leave.
He said the club weren't hiring and firing but I thought I was just wasting my time and told him that I doubted I would still be there at the end of the season. I got on with it and, sure enough, in the April I was gone.

BERNIE

You've been on the Three Legends radio show with me now for over 10 years and the listening figures have been fantastic. Obviously Micky Horswill has joined us since Eric Gates' departure. Is there a secret to its success?

MALCOLM

I think there is. I think that we don't take ourselves too seriously and the foundation of it is mickey taking.
I get the sense of the old Fulham dressing room when I'm in the radio studio. If we get down to a serious football subject then we really get our teeth into it. But what happens between the serious subjects is never that serious. So we are winding each other up all of the while and it's competitive in the way that we wind each other up.
We are there representing our club and we are attacking the other clubs. It's all very competitive but its all down to mickey taking. That's how you score your points and if you remember back, for the first six or eight weeks that we were on air with Eric, the callers were few and far between.
The reason for that, I think, is they were just sitting back wondering what was going on. It was something else. And it needed them to take those six to eight weeks, listening very carefully, to get to understand what was actually happening. Now the first thing the caller does when he comes on is take the mickey doesn't he?

BERNIE

Of course.

MALCOLM

With the vast majority of callers there's a verbal punch on the nose for all of us, or one of us at least, and they picked it up. They sussed it out very quickly and after those six to eight weeks they were on in their droves. Because that's basically what football thrives on, mickey taking.

BERNIE

Despite your personal glories, does it still rankle with you that you never actually won a major trophy?

MALCOLM

To a degree. I think it's one of those things. I see far, far lesser players winning trophies and I think it's good for them. It's just being in the right club at the right time. I made my mark on the game because I was there. It would have always been nice to win more caps, score more goals, win trophies. No, I'm grateful for the opportunity I had in the game.

BERNIE

Finally, Newcastle United in the last few years have been in turmoil. What do you blame for their demise?

MALCOLM

Well, you have always got to go to the top.
Other factors come into play, but I sensed that everything was going well under Bobby Robson's management. Then all of a sudden having finished third they didn't buy a single player in the summer. They got Lee Bowyer on a free transfer when that was the time for investment.

Newcastle have gone downhill ever since.

BERNIE

Can you see them recovering?

MALCOLM

It will take a decade and a whole amount of investment, which is difficult in the current financial climate.
So I think it will take a very long time before Newcastle will ever be seriously back in the title race. Think back. Newcastle United finished third under Bobby Robson. Six years ago when people were talking of the top three, Newcastle were part of that.

England manager don Revie talks tactics Supermac

HONOURS

Malcolm Ian Macdonald

PLAYING CAREER HISTORY

1968-1969 Fulham
1969-1971 Luton Town
1971-1976 Newcastle
1976-1979 Arsenal
1979   Djurgardens

MANAGERIAL CAREER HISTORY

1980-1984 Fulham
1987-1988 Huddersfield Town

CAPS 14 Full caps for England

Supermac in full flow for Newcastle

"Was it good management on his part or was it good luck? I still don't know to this day but I tell you what, it worked!"

Referring to newcastle manager Joe Harveys success

BOB MONCUR
NEWCASTLE

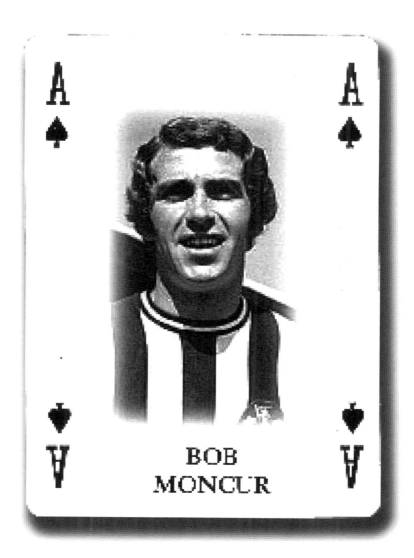

BOB
MONCUR

Bob Moncur was born on the 19th January 1945 in Perth Scotland.
Bob made his Newcastle debut at the tender age of 18 and after becoming a first team regular, he became captain of the magpise.
He was strong, read the game well, good in tackle and possesed leadership qualities.
I met captain Bob years ago while working for boro tv, I remember interviewing Bryan Robson on bobs boat.

I have done talk ins with him. Bob for me is a teriffic guy, he has no airs and graces, enjoys a laugh and of course lives and breathes Newcastle united. That for me is his only down side ha ha..

I had no problems meeting up with Bob to do this interview as he is working for the same radio station Real Radio North East.

The one thing I cant get my head around is that bob is the last Newcastle captain to lift a trophy, he lifted the Inter cities Fairs Cup and dear me that was way back in 1969.

BERNIE.

You were born in Perth in 1945. What kind of upbringing did you have?

BOB.

I had a good upbringing. My dad was a policeman, my mother was a housewife and I had a sister. We stayed there until I was nine, when we moved just outside Edinburgh to a place called Kirkliston. My dad became the chief inspector of salmon fishing in Scotland. Because he was a policeman and he used to do fishing he was ideal for the job. If you come across the Forth

Bridge, the first sign you'll see is Kirkliston, where Bob Moncur lived. I stayed there until I was 15, when of course I got involved in football.

BERNIE

As a kid was it always your ambition to become a professional footballer?

BOB

Initially I wanted to be a footballer. When I got on the Scottish football team I started off at left-back, even though I wasn't that big. I wasn't captain but by the time I'd finished I'd grown up and I was also playing centre half. Then they realised how good I was and made me skipper. I had all these scouts inviting me here and there and I went all over for seven, eight weeks. I was at Manchester United for three or four weeks. They couldn't make their mind up, then they decided I wasn't good enough. I got fed up with it all. You have to remember I was only 15 years of age. I went over it and discussed it with my dad. The police force was an option, because eventually I would have got my dad's job. It was like one of these jobs that stayed in the family, I would have been secure. It wasn't fantastic money, but a good, sturdy income. I had the choice and at one stage I thought I wasn't going to play football because at that age I was feeling down. Anyway, I came to Newcastle on trial and immediately loved it. I mean this sincerely. The people in the North East were just different people. They made me feel so welcome.
Plus the fact it was two and a bit hours down the road by car or train, so it was easy. Whereas if you go to the likes of Wolverhampton - where I could have gone - or to Manchester, in those days it was a long, long trip. I just felt so comfortable at Newcastle. So to answer your question, I did
have the ambition, I lost it and then I got it back again.

I came down here as a 15-year-old kid and stayed in digs.

BERNIE

Who was it who spotted you for Newcastle?

BOB

It was a guy called Jimmy Nellis and Charlie Mitten was the manager at the time. Charlie was quite an operator, and so was Jimmy. If you look at the records, it will actually say that I signed from Wishaw Juniors. I have never been to Wishaw in my life!

BERNIE

You made your first team debut in 1963 - any memories of that game?

BOB

Yes. It was against Luton. I was up against a guy called Ron Davies and we won. I quite enjoyed myself. I was a bit apprehensive before the game but I enjoyed it.

BERNIE

Who were your boyhood heroes?

BOB

Well, when I was living in Edinburgh I used to go to Hearts one week, Hibs the next. I just wanted to go and watch football. When I wasn't even 15 I used to get the bus and would sometimes jump on the supporters' bus from the local village.

My favourites then from Hearts were Willie Bauld, Dave Mackay . At Hibs it was players like Gordon Smith, Laurie Riley, Bobby Johnstone, George Young.

BERNIE

How would you describe your playing style?

BOB

Oh, fantastic! Seriously, I thought I was a good reader of the game. I certainly wasn't the quickest, in fact some people said I was slow. I was a good tackler, strong, and very seldom lost a tackle. I can honestly say I'm very proud of my career. While I was known as a bit of a hard man, I never got sent off in the whole of my career at any level.
I couldn't believe that I achieved that. Mind you, in those days you had to kill someone to get sent off! My strengths were that I kept cool, calm and collected. I wasn't the greatest player.
I wasn't a great passer but I was lucky to play with good players and I think I was a good skipper. I thought I was a good player, not a brilliant player. You wouldn't pay money to come and watch me.

BERNIE

I wouldn't pay money to watch any defender, not even Franz Beckenbauer! You went on to captain Newcastle. Did you feel any added pressure wearing the armband?

BOB

Well, don't forget I had captained the Scottish schoolboys team and every team I had played for, for some reason, made me skipper. Either I must have had qualities or maybe I shouted the loudest, but I was always pretty determined and didn't like getting beaten. Joe Harvey gave me the captaincy for the first time at Arsenal ahead of Frank Clark, of Nottingham Forest fame. He had watched me play in the Under-23 team up at Hampden Park against England and guys like Mick Channon, Brian Kidd. But he did it completely out of the blue. After announcing his team selection he just said: "By the way Bob, you're taking the ball out." Frank didn't like the way he did it and I had to accept it wasn't the best way to do it, but that's how I got the captaincy. Right out of the blue. Frank was a great vice captain and we played together for a lot of years. I was the one shouting and balling and he was a thinker.

Joe Harvey was a good man manager, but when it came to tactics he would just say: "Go out there and don't let them play. "You know, the usual things, just do what you're good at!"

BERNIE

What was your match day ritual?

BOB

When I got married in 1967 and we had our son Paul and daughter Angela, I had a strict routine. I had a split level house in Gateshead and on a Saturday morning I would lie in bed until about half past 11. I would get up and my mum and dad used to come down to look after the kids when Camille went to the match. When I got up I would have cornflakes and peaches, with the juice out of the can as well. If they weren't on the table, I wasn't a happy man. A dour Scot, that's what I was! Then I would get myself organised and jump in the car. There was Camille running around like a blue-arsed fly trying to organise two kids and I was ready to go. When I think back, I think how selfish I was, but that was my dedication, to be there early in case there was a traffic jam. I liked to get to St James' a good two hours before the game. In those days we used to drive there and we had a car parking space against the wall opposite the main entrance. But Camille and my father or whoever was with me had no place to go. There was no players' lounge or suites, so they had to sit in the car or go down town or whatever. On the freezing cold days all the girls would jump in one car and run the heater of the car to keep warm.

That was the life of the WAG as they are called nowadays, no facilities and sitting in a car. After games it could be an hour and a half before we were out after talking to the press boys.There was no players' bar or anything like that

BERNIE

How do you compare your wages to what modern day players earn?

BOB

When I look back I think I was on a decent wage, but it was nothing like the current era. The best wage I ever got was when I finished at Sunderland in 1976. We had just got promotion and I got a £50 rise, which took me up to 325 quid a week. If you took the working man's wage back then, and that's the way to do it, I was probably getting three or four times more than the average. Nowadays I couldn't even do the calculations!

BERNIE

In 1969 you lifted the Fairs Cup against Ujpest Dozsa. For non-Newcastle fans, who did you beat on the way?

BOB

The first game was against Feyenoord and we beat them 4-0 at St James' Park. I didn't play as I had just had my cartilage out. Feyenoord were top dogs at the time, the cream of Europe. Even though I was skipper I stood in the paddock and watched the game. That's the way it was back then. When we played over there and I wasn't fit, I wasn't even invited to travel with the squad. I ended up going with the supporters' club and sat in the stand watching the team. You would have thought they would pay for the skipper to come. It was unbelievable when I look back now. The next tie was Sporting from Portugal and then we beat Real Zaragoza from Spain. The first leg over there was on New Year's Day and we lost 3-2 in a fantastic game. We beat them back at St James' Park to go through and then faced Vitoria Setubal in the quarter-finals back in the stadium where we had played Sporting Lisbon. It was probably one of the most frightening experiences I've ever had in football.

There was a big track around the pitch and there were blokes with clowns' heads going round on motorbikes. The noise with all of the hooters was unreal and they were obviously trying to upset us. We had already beaten them 5-1 at Newcastle so they were trying to pull all sorts of tricks and it was a bit of a dirty game. I remember shouting 'let's get out of here' when I was going down the tunnel after the game. It was hostile, there was police everywhere and people throwing things. Alan Foggon was a Jack the Lad and had been giving a few people a bit of gyp through the game and was still on the pitch arguing with people. I can't repeat what I said when I went back out to get him but by then the crowd were all on the pitch and coming towards us. The police weren't doing anything. When we backed off towards the tunnel we walked into the back of the net so we couldn't go anywhere and ended up hitting a few blokes before running down the tunnel! Rangers were next up in the semi-finals and I could see some of our Scots boys who had played up

there and were used to getting hammered by them were intimidated when we walked out at Ibrox. I actually said to them that they were playing for Newcastle now, not Partick Thistle, because we had a decent side. I gave them an ear bashing and told them I was confident we would beat them.
We got a draw and beat them 2-0 down at St James' and that was us in the final.

BERNIE

Not only did you captain the side in the Fairs Cup final, you scored a hat-trick. How did you manage that being a centre half, Bob?

BOB

Don't forget, when I first started at Newcastle I came as a left back. The first game I ever played for Newcastle they played me at outside left. I scored six goals and we won about 12. I continued at outside left in the youth team and we won the Youth Cup in 1961. It was the first time Newcastle had ever won it. So I had actually scored some goals. I was good at volleys and I had two good feet and used to work hard on my left foot. There is a good story behind that for young kids.
I wasn't the most mobile and eventually got moved back to centre half, but went on to captain Scotland. We left Newcastle with a 3-0 advantage but Ujpest were a cracking side and we got slaughtered over there in the first half and were 2-0 down. Joe Harvey really got a grip of us at half-time because our heads were down, mine included. Joe bundled through the door like John Wayne with a cigarette in his mouth and basically told us to score a goal, because we hadn't been over the halfway line. He said: "I'm telling you, f****** foreigners, score a goal and they will collapse like a pack of cards."

He wished us good luck before leaving us and within five or six minutes of going back out we got a corner kick and I volleyed one in. It was like a perfect golf shot That made it 2-1 and we actually went on to beat them 3-2 on the night. We got the cup and ran around the pitch and were celebrating in the far end with the fans. The champagne flowed in the dressing room afterwards and when Joe burst in with his cigarette he said: "What did I f****** tell you!"

Was it good management on his part or was it good luck? I still don't know to this day but I tell you what, it worked!

BERNIE

You won your first Scotland cap against Holland. Who was manager at the time?

BOB

Bobby Brown of Rangers fame. Jimmy Smith played that night, Jinky, who eventually came to Newcastle.

BERNIE

Did the call-up come as a surprise or did you expect it?

BOB

Well, it sort of came out of the blue a little bit. The problem I had with playing at Newcastle since I was 15 was I honestly don't think they realised I was Scottish, because I had been down here since I was a kid. But Bobby Brown gave me my first cap and then after that when I was playing for the national team I was made skipper.

BERNIE

You represented the tartan on 16 occasions. Should it have been more?

BOB

Yes. I was unlucky because I was skipper, then I got an injury. Each time I got an injury there was a change of manager. Tommy Docherty brought me back after I didn't play in the home internationals series because of injury. Tommy knew the English scene because he had been at Manchester United. But then Willie Ormond came in as manager of Scotland and that was the end of my international career.

BERNIE

In 1974 you led Newcastle United to Wembley and the FA Cup final against Liverpool. You got gubbed 3-0, what went wrong that day?

BOB

To me our 1969 team was a really good team. We weren't the best of players but we were really good pros and we all knew our weaknesses. The '74 team was a better team than that, but we had a few prima donnas, different personalities or whatever you want to call them. On the day we could have beaten Liverpool if we performed the way we normally did. We had players like Terry McDermott, Alan Kennedy and Malcolm Macdonald. On the day certain players didn't perform and that's why we got gubbed.

BERNIE

We obviously know Malcolm - did he leave his shooting boots behind that day?

BOB

Don't wind me up Bernie! Some of the talk was that we were going to do this and that to Liverpool. The likes of myself who had been at Wembley were telling the lads to keep quiet and let's be underdogs and get on with it, because they had no idea what it was like. But certain stuff was all over the papers and all the Liverpool manager Bill Shankly was doing was cutting out the stories and sticking them up in their dressing room. Alan Kennedy had called Tommy Smith an old bugger or something like that and on the day Smithy gave Alan an earful.
There was nothing Alan could say, was there?

BERNIE

On the subject of defeats and cups, you were part of the Newcastle team famously beaten by Hereford in the FA Cup.

BOB

Yeah, yeah, yeah!

BERNIE

Does that still rankle with you even now?

BOB

In my defence Bernie, the first leg was at St James' Park and we got a draw. If I would have been playing in the first game it wouldn't have been a draw. I was out injured and when I came back it was my first game for a long, long time. We went down to Hereford and it was a total disaster. When we got there the pitch was waterlogged. Instead of coming home we stayed there and it was still waterlogged the next night. We had to stay there for about a week and had to go to Marks and Spencer to buy underwear. Don't forget, we only went for one game and all of a sudden we were staying down there, because Hereford was a long way in those days. If the truth is known, we actually slaughtered them in the first half but we just couldn't put the ball in the back of the net and of course their goal was just out of the blue.

BERNIE

The Cup final was your last appearance for the black and whites. Did that come as a surprise?

BOB

No, it was my choice. I had been at Newcastle for 14 years, nine or 10 of them as skipper, and I was just getting to the stage where I needed a new challenge. I wasn't as happy with the team. I was getting older and we were getting younger people who had ideas. It was a fact there was a split in the camp and I thought I didn't need it and needed a change.

Bob Stokoe was a family friend and I used to play golf with him. He used to play for Newcastle of course, but he was managing Sunderland. He asked me on a couple of occasions if I would go down and play for them but I was always a Newcastle player. But then we got to the final and lost and I felt I'd had enough. I phoned Stokoe up and said it was time for me to move, so I went to Sunderland.

BERNIE

Was it a difficult decision with Newcastle and Sunderland being such fierce rivals?

BOB

I knew it wasn't the most popular decision in the world. I didn't want to move from where I was living. The kids were happy and Sunderland were doing okay. They were in the Second Division at the time. Stokoe said he wanted me to help Sunderland get promotion and that was my motivation. The first year we failed on goal average or a point. We had to beat Aston Villa down there and we only got a draw. Then the next year we had won the championship just after Easter. That's how easy it was, it wasn't like it is now. I recall the first time driving into Roker Park for a pre-season friendly. People were being really nasty towards me. Fingers were pointed and bricks were coming at me. Stokoe in his wisdom had me skipper as well over Bobby Kerr, who had just captained Sunderland to FA Cup final victory in 1973. It was tough enough being an ex-Newcastle player. But I was one of the first players to have a sponsored car when I was at Newcastle and when we won the FA Cup semi-final it was decorated in black and white stripes and called The Geordie Special. I was thinking they were a bit nasty at Sunderland but then I realised I'd driven into Roker Park in it!
I went to the car dealership the next day and said: "Paint it red will you!"

BERNIE

After two years you left Sunderland and joined Carlisle, how did that go?

BOB

After Sunderland were crowned Second Division champions in 1976 I joined Carlisle as manager. Sunderland had been relegated after just one season back in the top flight, Jim Montgomery and I were dropped and Stokoe had gone by then. Ian MacFarlane was in charge and instead of Sunderland sticking with the old heads, we were on our way out and Carlisle invited me to manage, not to play. Having got there, they were looking dead and buried. I decided that I was the best player they had got, so I played.
I think I played 11 or 12 games and we just missed out on staying up by
goal average. They were dead and buried when I arrived, then we went on a great run. It would have been a great achievement if I could have kept them up.

BERNIE

You not only managed Carlisle, you managed Hearts, Plymouth and Hartlepool. How did you find management as opposed to playing? Was it something you always wanted to do?

BOB

Well, the first three teams you mentioned, that was all part of the plan. Joe Harvey had said to me that I had to go away and learn the business and come back to Newcastle. So I went to Carlisle and had four great years there and got a bit impatient. That was when I signed Peter Beardsley and Hearts came and head hunted me. Don't forget, I supported them and they were a big club in Edinburgh. We were only getting seven or 8,000 at Carlisle crowd-wise. We were doing quite well but I was getting bored. I joined Hearts but it was a bad move. We were in a terrific mess, it was worse than I had anticipated. We got promotion that year against all the odds but I knew we were going to get relegated the following year.

We had no money and I just went for kids and brought in John Robertson, Gary Mackay and David Bowman.

All three went on to play for Scotland and Robertson went on to play for Newcastle. Wallace Mercer took over the reigns at Tynecastle and I have to say he did a great job for Hearts. But I could never have worked for Wallace because there would have been too much intrusion from the directors.

I wanted to be in charge of my team affairs and fortunately Plymouth came in for me. When I arrived at Plymouth the two guys in charge were taking over as well. I worked with them for a year and I didn't enjoy it. They knew nothing about football. I had been putting up with them, if you like, and I decided I had had enough of football. I had been in football for a lot of years and I thought there was more to life. I was getting involved with sailing and loved it and that had a lot to do with my decision.

When I returned to the North East I enjoyed playing squash and ended up buying a squash club. I stayed there for four years then sold it. John Smart, who was chairman at Hartlepool, then asked me to go to Pools and manage.

I'd known John for years - a nice man, football fanatic - and told him I was finished and had had enough. He phoned me again about 18 months later and I ended up going to Hartlepool, and I can honestly say to do John a favor.

We did quite well and the following season I went on my boat and sailed to Spain. It had always been my ambition.

I returned to Pools after my sail in the summer and resigned and that was me out of it.

BERNIE

You mentioned you like sailing. You have a catamaran don't you?

BOB

Yes, over in the Grenadines, in St Vincent just south of St Lucia in the Caribbean. You can see some fantastic scenery. It's the most wonderful place to sail and it can be quite challenging as well. It's not claustrophobic and it's a great little boat.

BERNIE

So you are captain of the boat and you take people out, is that right?

BOB

I got the business together and I got five partners involved, so six of us on the boat. They were just doing it for their holidays. My plan was to have so many weeks and I will take people sailing, but the whole business was set up. Obviously I had to raise the money, get partners in. We picked up the boat from Cape Town in South Africa and I sailed it all the way across the South Atlantic and into St Vincent where it is now, over 6,500 miles away.

BERNIE

You obviously love it. Is it better than football?

BOB

I love every minute of it. When I was playing football I loved it, but it was my business then. But when I got into sailing every sail is different and I still love sailing.

BERNIE

You're still involved at St James' Park on match day, hosting one of the boxes, and of course doing the games summarising on Real Radio. Do you enjoy both?

BOB

The thing about me is I love meeting people. I love being an honorary player and I have just kept my feet on the ground. I like to think I have got time for most people and I like the banter and involvement because there is no pressure on me. The commentary with Justin Lockwood is fantastic because he's the young buck and he is full of enthusiasm and I'm the kind of old cynic.

BERNIE

You had a health scare a few years ago with cancer. Has that made you appreciate things a bit more or have you always appreciated things?

BOB

I've never taken anything for granted. I wouldn't like to think I have been a Flash Harry. I love my golf. I love the sailing, so I think I have been very lucky in my lifestyle. I have also played and coached squash. I have led a privileged lifestyle.

BERNIE

I must ask you about the state of Newcastle United in the last couple of years.

BOB

I'm concerned. I have watched Newcastle United go from the really high days and now we have gone a long way back. You think, we were challenging for the Premiership under Kevin Keegan and recently we've been relegated before thankfully bouncing back into the Premier League thanks to Chris Hughton and his team. I am disappointed and I feel helpless at times, albeit I genuinely think I could advise occasionally.
But so far I have never been asked, which disappoints me a little bit. I have been involved with Newcastle for 48 years. I'm now a supporter, I have been through the management scene, the player scene and I just feel I could have something to offer in some way because it's our club. Mike Ashley owns it at this minute and I'm not anti Mike Ashley. I think the guy has come in and tried to do what he could.
He didn't come in wanting things to go wrong, he has not done anything intentionally wrong. There is no doubting there have been mistakes made by other boards, which I could see coming. You think: "Why don't you pick the phone up and ask me?" Some of the players we have bought, the minute I see them I think they have got no chance. You can see that at Middlesbrough and it just disappoints me. We have thrown millions and millions of pounds away. Part of my strengths were I was a good buyer and a good seller. I had to do that to survive at Carlisle and Plymouth.

BERNIE

Do you feel sorry for the fans?

BOB

I feel devastated for them - it's 40 years since we won a trophy.

Okay, they have had a few highs with cup finals. Sir Bobby got them going, as did Kevin. But there has been more bad years than good. I feel sorry for the punters. For some of the fans it is their life.

BERNIE

Is there anything you would change in your career?

BOB

I wouldn't have left Carlisle and gone to Hearts, that was a mistake. When I was there the Newcastle job came up but they would have had to pay compensation. Nothing happened for two or three weeks, then I phoned John Gibson from the Evening Chronicle and asked what was going on. He said that the board weren't prepared to pay compensation and I said:
"Well, I will tell you what, you can tell them to stick the job up their arse."
Then I put the phone down and that was me finished in terms of managing Newcastle United.

BERNIE

So was that a big regret?

BOB

I would have loved to have gone to Newcastle, but not under those circumstances.
My reason was if they were not prepared to pay £35,000 and I'm buying and selling players for £150,000, what chance have I got as a manager?

BERNIE

Who was the best and most professional player you played alongside?

BOB

One of the best was my boyhood pal David Craig at right back, just a class full back. When I came down here as a kid, I was always struggling and scrapping. Davie was a Rolls Royce from day one, he was always going to make the grade. Malcolm Macdonald was obviously an exciting player and great to play with, although we had our differences.

BERNIE

That's well documented. Was it a clash of egos, you as captain and him a big name striker?

BOB

I didn't have an ego. To be fair, we wanted the same thing - success. There was loads of stories about us having fights and all the rest of it. We used to have arguments on the training field. I can't ever remember punching him, but I probably did.
But that is all forgotten. Both of us are passionate. I had no problem with that. But probably the most exciting player I ever played with - and there were loads of them - was Tony Green. Tony Green became a legend in 37 games at Newcastle.

BERNIE

He is a guy I would love to meet. Not because he played for Newcastle, but because he played for Albion Rovers!

BOB

When we played England at Hampden Park, Tony came on as a sub and got man of the match for Scotland.

BERNIE

Going back to Malcolm, and not to wind you up, he arrived at Newcastle in a Rolls Royce. Were the players aware of that?

BOB

We didn't see that. If we did, we would have been saying: "Who's that flash bastard?"

BERNIE

Can you believe that Newcastle United have not won a domestic trophy in over 56 years?

BOB

I can't and I would have never imagined it. Newcastle are still a big club, unfortunately probably not for the right reasons. Fifty-two thousand paying punters, Middlesbrough would love that.

BERNIE

Recently you were given the Freedom of Gateshead. How big an honour was that and were you surprised with the fantastic turn out?

BOB

I have lived in Gateshead for 30 years and been in the home I'm
in now for 25 years. I have got a couple of good friends who
work in the council who are football fans as well and I have just
got to know them. We have done a few things together, nothing
sensational, but I very rarely have said no to them. I tried to
make an effort, because I want to give the public and punters
something back. So to be given the Freedom of Gateshead, I was
very proud and privileged and felt a bit humble as well.
Some of the guys that turned up, Brendan Foster, Jonathan
Edwards, Mike Neville, yourself and Sir Bobby Robson, it was
fantastic. I'm proud to live in Gateshead.

With the fairs cup.

HONOURS

ROBERT MONCUR

PLAYING CAREER HISTORY
1962-1974 Newcastle United
1974-1977 Sunderland
1977   Carlisle United

PLAYING CAREER HONOURS (winners)
Newcastle
1969 Fairs Cup.

MANAGERIAL CAREER HISTORY

1976-1986 Carlisle United
1980-1981 Heart of Midlothian
1981-1983 Plymouth Argyle
1988-1989 Hartlepool

CAPS 16 Full caps for Scotland.

Smile bob your on camera!

"To be given a knighthood is exceptionally special. Going to the ceremony, that thrill has to be the second greatest day of your life. The greatest day is when you are born"

Referring to his knighthood.

SIR BOBBY ROBSON
NEWCASTLE

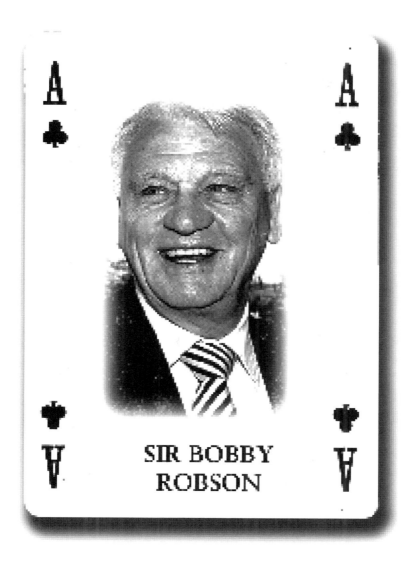

SIR BOBBY
ROBSON

Robert William Robson, Sir Bobby as he is know was born on 18th Febuary 1933, Sacriston, County Durham
Over the years , I have had the privilege and the pleasure of meeting Sir Bobby,
Sadly he passed away in 2009.

I wasn't fortunate enough to interview Sir Bobby myself but Real Radio Pete Graves did. I have been given permission to include it in this book.

PETE

Sir Bobby, you're a legend in North East football. As a youngster did you ever think you would have such a great career?

SIR BOBBY

No, I didn't think that I would ever hit the jackpot, but I always wanted to be a professional footballer from maybe the age of 10. I loved the game and played it every night in the back streets with my mates. Football always came first before homework. I fell in love with the game early on and never fell out of love with it. I couldn't wait until I was 17, when I knew that I could sign pro for somebody. I didn't know who, I just hoped that by that time I was good enough.

PETE

When did the opportunity arise to become a professional?

SIR BOBBY

I played for Langley Park Juniors and had caught the eye. I
suppose I was a bit of a prodigy. The North East was full of
talent scouts from all of the clubs in the country, not just
Newcastle and Sunderland. When I was 17 I could have signed
for Blackpool, Sheffield Wednesday and Lincoln City. I was
already on schoolboy forms with Middlesbrough.
Sunderland chased me, so did Newcastle and Arsenal were also
interested in me at the time. I had a big decision to make about
where to go and Fulham eventually signed me.

PETE

Why Fulham?

SIR BOBBY

It was simple and I always remembered it when I became a
manager years later. Fulham's manager in 1950 was Bill Dodgin
and he travelled up from London to come to our house. He sat in
my parents' sitting room and more or less would not leave until
he persuaded my mother and father that Fulham was the club for
their son. He also persuaded me he was a genuine man and he
made the effort to sign me. Newcastle and all the other clubs
sent their local scout and that had a big bearing on me.
When I became manager of Ipswich years later we had no
money and were always in the market for young players.
I used to have scouts all over the country and we found lots and
lots of great young players, like Terry Butcher and Mick Mills.
Whenever I was told there was a special player in a certain part
of the country I always made a point of going to the boy's home,
see his parents and persuade them that the club was right for
their son, or invite them all down to Ipswich

PETE

A lot of players described you as a father figure.

SIR BOBBY

I think it's very important how you manage your players, how you talk to them, how you can persuade them to be what they are and do what you want them to do. And I think the more time you spend, the better rapport you have. You build up a terrific relationship and it stood me in good stead.
I learned that from Bill Dodgin and I used it all through my life. When I wanted to sign the two Dutch players for Ipswich, Arnold Muhren and Frans Thijssen, I flew to Holland and met both players' parents and wives. I had to have a kind of love affair with the wives to persuade them to leave the country. So that was always in my makeup, that's how I was, and I know Sir Alex Ferguson does this as well. There is no better person than the man at the top trying to sign a player.
I prided myself on that and players do sign for the manager as well as the club if he is a good guy. That's why over the years we did sign a lot of players, and a lot of great young players that didn't cost the club money. It paid handsome dividends.

PETE

What was sit like playing for England as a young lad from Langley Park?

SIR BOBBY

It was the moment of my life really, a dream come true. I was at West Bromwich at the time, playing in a very good team.
In those days you found out through the paper, no phone calls or letter of authenticity from the Football Association. I learned of

my first selection for England for the match against France in November 1957 in one of the local Birmingham papers. There it was in the evening sports paper under a 'stop press' notice - I was one of the XI.

PETE

Were you surprised when you saw your name on that list?

SIR BOBBY

No, not really. I was playing very well at the time and my name had been thrown in by journalists as one of the candidates for the team. So I always knew that once the paper had you down as one of the possibilities there was always a chance.
Walter Winterbottom was the England manager at the time. He was a wonderful man and my mentor really in many ways.
It was a team in those days, not a squad. There were no substitutes and if you got an injury in a match you struggled on. Or if two went off injured, you played on with nine men.

PETE

How did your England debut go? Were you nervous?

SIR BOBBY

Yes, I was to be honest. I remember asking the great Tom Finney what it was going to be like and he said it was going to be difficult. He said the French team would be very powerful and were the best players in France. But he also said I had to remember that I was playing with the best players in England as well. Then he told me that if I got a bit weary to pass the ball to him and he would keep it for 10 minutes until I got my confidence back! He made me laugh. That was the sort of player he was and he was that sort of player if it went well.

We won 4-0. I scored twice on my debut and Tom Taylor scored twice as well. There was a certain irony about my debut. Some of the team was comprised of Manchester United's famous players the Busby Babes, like Duncan Edwards. They were wonderful players and three months later they died in the Munich plane crash disaster.

My first game for England was the last for some of those players and I always lived with that. I never forgot it.

Bobby Charlton, if you remember, survived. He was on the plane. Bobby came into the England team and I played with him for several years. From time to time during our meetings we used to talk about some of those

players, like Eddie Coleman, David Pegg and what a tragedy that was for England. And it was tough luck really on Walter Winterbottom as well because we had qualified for the World Cup with many of the Manchester United team, they were great players. Tommy Taylor was a fantastic striker and Duncan Edwards would potentially have been one of the most powerful players you would ever see in your life.

Half the team got wiped out. We went to the World Cup in Sweden in 1958 with not the best team and got to the quarter-finals. We would have been a much better team with the Busby Babes in it.

PETE

Italia 90 was a time when the country really got to know and love you. What are your memories of being England manager - the highs and lows?

SIR BOBBY

I can remember everything. Yes, there were highs and lows.

I was there for eight years over two World Cups and was very proud of course to be given the opportunity.

PETE

Do you think because you had to operate on such a tight budget at Ipswich, that was what helped you become a great manager?

SIR BOBBY

Without doubt. The 14 years I had at Ipswich was a marvellous experience. I ran the club on a pretty thin budget. We didn't have any money, it was run on a youth policy and we bought well. I spent every penny as though it was my money and we had to be right, couldn't make a mistake. For 10 of those years Ipswich played in Europe, so I had a great European experience. I took little Ipswich to the likes of Barcelona and Real Madrid. You name it, we went there. And we won the European Cup in 1981 with a very good team. The very first book I wrote on football was about Ipswich Town and I called it 'Time On The Grass'. It was the amount of time we spent with the players in training on the grass and we made schoolboys into internationals. People like Terry Butcher, John Wark, Eric Gates and George Burley. It wasn't luck, it was hard work. Continued good preparation and that old saying, 'practice makes perfect'. After about three years when I sort of proved my point they gave me a 10-year contract. Nobody gets that now.

PETE

Italia 90 was the closest England had come since 1966 to winning the World Cup.

SIR BOBBY

We haven't got that far since then. We had got to the quarter-final stage and I fell at the semi-final stage as a manager. I had a good team, it was as simple as that. We had a strong mentality, good team morale, some great players and everybody knew their jobs. We also had a good balance. I liked width and we had wingers in John Barnes and Chris Waddle. Gary Linkeker and Peter Beardsley weren't giants up front so we had to play ground football. Our style was like Arsenal play at the moment - balls into feet, one-twos and thread the ball through gaps. Peter was quick but his mind was quicker. He saw openings before they were there. Paul Gascoigne obviously came into the limelight. He was quite sensational, such a major talent. Bryan Robson was a terrific captain. A great tackler and example to everyone. Terry Butcher was similar. He was a warrior and a defender who loved to defend. And in Peter Shilton we had one of the world's best goalkeepers. So everything was right. The balance, the shape, the quality. It was going to take a very good team to knock us out but we didn't get knocked out, we basically lost on penalties. If you were to ask me what was the greatest misery of my life, that would be it - the night we lost on penalties. We had some great penalty kickers as well. The five we had chosen were equal to anybody in the country. Stuart Pearce was a great player and penalty taker and he missed the crucial fourth penalty. Chris Waddle took the fifth and he was a great penalty taker. He could score them in training with his eyes closed. For the fifth penalty he just sort of leaned back and hit it high and wide. One minute we were in front to win and kill the semi final off, the next minute we were out. I had a great career after my England job. Barcelona was unexplainable, I loved Newcastle, Porto, all those clubs. I had a great time at PSV because it was a properly run club, a gentleman's club run by top notch people. But if you were to ask me what was my greatest and worst time in football, it would be that one England match in the semi-final of the World Cup against Germany. We went out trying to follow Sir Alf Ramsey's success in the 1966 World Cup. We knew we had a great chance and it was so disappointing when we lost.

PETE

The whole nation wept with you on that night.

SIR BOBBY

My bucket of tears was bigger than anybody else's, I'll tell you. I got over it, as you have to. The saddest moment was in the dressing room afterwards trying to tell Chrissy Waddle and Stuart Pearce that it didn't matter, to get their heads up. They knew it did matter. But they were great characters those two and they took it on the chin. They wanted to take the penalties. Lots of people would fight and say they wanted to take number eight or 11, not number four or five. I had a nothing but a great depth of feeling for them and I never forgot them. They were distraught.

PETE

Thousands welcomed you when you came back to Newcastle as manager. Did you ever dream about returning to your home town club?

SIR BOBBY

To be honest, I never thought I would come back home. It was almost 50 years from the day I left to the day I came back.

It was never my intention. I had two jobs with Ipswich and England for 22 years and then I went abroad for 10 years. I finished PSV to retire but I didn't really want to. And on the first Saturday of not working for 50 years I didn't like it. I said to my wife Elsie on the first Saturday of the season how much I didn't like it and I was never going to go into the supermarket on a Saturday afternoon ever again. I didn't know what was next in line, but then Ruud Gullit dismissed himself from Newcastle and the job became available. I didn't apply for the job, I just kept reading the papers every day and suddenly read that I was one of the contenders. I was in my 60s but I had a brilliant mind and great health. Then I got a call saying they were very interested to talk to me about the Newcastle position and would I be prepared to meet them in London? I got to London in about two-and-a-half minutes, met them and agreed on a formal contract. I was overjoyed. I didn't know how good it would be but I loved absolutely every minute of it. Newcastle were in deep trouble and I remember the chairman Freddie Shepherd telling me that I had a very difficult job on my hands and he wasn't sure I could do it. That's what he said to me. I've told the story many times.

I think everybody thought that we were going down. Their worry was that we were going to drop out of the Premiership, not only into the First Division but into the Second Division. They thought the club was in free fall and we stabilised it. We didn't have any money either by the way. That was the second thing Freddie Shepherd said to me.

PETE

That first home game against Sheffield Wednesday heralded your arrival in pure Bobby Robson fashion - an 8-0 win.

SIR BOBBY

It was a miracle really and an amazing scoreline. Alan Shearer hadn't been in the team but I brought him back and he got five that day. I think at one time he thought his career was about to finish, but he played another five years with me and two more with Graeme Souness and broke Jackie Milburn's scoring record. I thought I would last for two year and get kicked out for some reason but I stayed five years and put the club in the top echelon of the league the last three years.

It wasn't easy. I took over an alien side and in my last three years we finished third, fourth and fifth. We are a club who should be in the top six always. We've got a wonderful stadium and an even better public and a sell out at every match. They know there football up here and it's a place that really does need some success and it deserves it as well, because we've got an amazing sporting public. I'm not being boastful or egotistical but I put us up there with Chelsea, Liverpool, Manchester United and Arsenal.

PETE

You've got a great relationship with the Geordie public.

SIR BOBBY

Hopefully I have, but it's easy because I'm one of them. I was born and bred here and my father took me to the club when I was a kid. When I was 14 I used to be with my father at 10am outside Newcastle's gates to be first into the ground. Of course I remember Ronaldo from my time at Barcelona. Figo when I was at Sporting, Guardiola at Barcelona and Romario at PSV. But all my heroes were Newcastle heroes and Jackie Milburn was my all-time favourite. As I said, my father introduced me to Newcastle and it's really been the love of my life. Barcelona

213

was exciting, a thrill. You don't get that job unless you're something special. Not that I was special, but I did a good job abroad and I won things with them. But the five years I had back among my own folk and at my father's club would be the prize above anything else. My father went to work white and came back black, because he was a coal miner for 52 years. So in terms of emotion and warmth and getting the club out of trouble and up the table was a thrill for me.

Freddie Shepherd was a chairman who always tried to find money for the manager and I became Freeman of the City, which was a big thrill for me.

You don't get much better than that honour. I just couldn't believe it had happened to me.

PETE

What about your knighthood? You must have been delighted?

SIR BOBBY

Yes, I was. I didn't expect it when it was announced. I really got the shock of my life. I wondered how they arrived at me, but I suppose I did serve the game with distinction for over 50 years and I was quite a good ambassador for the country because I worked abroad and enjoyed success.

To be given a knighthood is exceptionally special. Going to the ceremony, that thrill has to be the second greatest day of your life. The greatest day is when you are born.

PETE

Any regrets looking back?

SIR BOBBY

No, none at all. I was obviously very sorry when I lost my job at Newcastle, but that's the name of the game. Better football managers than me have lost their jobs, but I'd do it all again. I've no regrets. I set out to be a footballer and when I was halfway through my career I knew I wanted to stay in the game and become a coach, then a manager. I never left the coaching side behind. Some do and I don't understand that. I wanted to be on the pitch every day with the players. I probably achieved some things that I though at 14 years of age would be beyond me. I played for and managed England and wanted to get better and moved abroad for a wonderful experience with different players, languages, mentalities and cultures.
I went to Barcelona when I was 63 and couldn't speak a word of Spanish. When I look back, that was frightening.
Sometimes I look back over my life and scratch my head and wonder how I did certain things. I spent the first six months at Barcelona running a football club and hardly talking to the players. That's where Jose Mourinho came in. I needed an interpreter and he was with me at Porto and I took him to Barcelona with me. Later on I could push him aside and conduct my own affairs with the players. I just had the most unbelievable and wonderful life and there's only one game I can thank for all that - football. It has been my angel, my saviour, the whole works.

PETE

Finally, how important are your wife Elsie and your faith?

SIR BOBBY

You can't achieve anything without your family. I've been married for 52 years now to someone who was a Sunderland supporter when she was a young girl. Can you believe that? She worked at Sunderland Infirmary as a nurse and we lived life to the full. We have got three glorious sons doing well in good jobs. They have been my bedrock. They say behind every man there has to be a great woman, and that's the case with Elsie for sure. She lets me do my thing. She didn't really want to go abroad but I said we were going and she packed her bags and we went on the understanding it was for two years. We ended up staying for 10, so without her and my family I couldn't have done it. My father and mother were alive for quite some time and my father saw me become manager of England. That was a great day for him. I wish he had been alive when I became the manager of Newcastle because he would have done somersaults! He saw great days when I was at Ipswich. Unfortunately he died before I went abroad so he didn't see my Barcelona days. But I'm sure someone will have told him up there. Without my family's support and the way my parents brought me up, I would never have achieved what I did

One of the most respected men in the game

HONOURS

ROBERT WILLIAM ROBSON.

PLAYING CAREER HISTORY

1950-1956 Fulham
1956-1962 West Bromwich Albion
1962-1967 Fulham
1967-1968 Vancouver Royals

MANAGERIAL CAREER HISTORY

1968 Fulham
1969-1982 Ipswich
1982-1990 England
1990-1992 PSV Eindhoven
1992-1994 Sporting CP
1994-1996 Porto
1996-1997 Barcelona
1998-1999 PSV Eindhoven
1999-2004 Newcastle United.

MANAGERIAL CAREER HONOURS(winners)

Ipswich
1973 Texaco cup
1978 FA Cup
1981UEFA Cup
England
1986,88,89 Rous Cup
PSV Eindhoven
1991/92 Dutch championship

218

Porto
1994 Cup of Portugal
1995, 1996 Portugese championship.
Barcelona
1996 Spanish super cup
1997 Copa Del Rey
1997 European Cup winners cup

CAPS 20 full caps for England.

Bobby Robson ,CBE, OBE

Sir Bobby shows his ball skills.

"I mean, he was great to know. He was my best friend and I'd do it all again. But he knackered my career up."

Referring to George Best.

MICKY HORSWILL
SUNDERLAND

MICKY
HORSWILL

Michael Frederick Horswill, was born 6th March 1953 in Anfield Plain Durham. He played for Sunderland, Man City, Plymouth Argyle, Hull City, Carlisle and Happy Valley in Hong Kong.

He started his career at his hometown club Sunderland aged 12. He signed professional forms and made his first team debut against Preston North End in a 3-1 victory in April 1972. He was a central midfield, more defensive, hard working no nonsence tackler. He reveled in midfield scraps.

I had met Micky over the years mostly in nightclubs like Hardwick Hall and Tall Trees Yarm. Since he joined the Legends show in 2006 we have become very close. I said on air that his nickname at Sunderland was 'The Tiddler,' I said he got called it when he jumped in the communal bath. Needless to say the name has stuck.

I find Micky, dry, funny and full of life a great mate who will always help you out.

BERNIE

You were born and bred in Annfield Plain, Durham. What kind of upbringing did you have?

MICK

A very simple upbringing. My dad was a driver. He worked for Schweppes actually, next door to where we work at Team Valley. He was there for 22 years. My mother was a cleaner, she worked in the council offices and that. I have four sisters and so they worked all their lives to keep us clothed and fed. So it was a very simple, basic life.

BERNIE

They tell me your sisters were better at football than you!

MICK

Yeah (laughs). Every one of them was better than me!

BERNIE

You joined Sunderland as a kid of 12 before signing apprentice forms at 15. How difficult was it progressing through the ranks? Any of the other kids progress into the first team?

MICK

I'm not trying to be funny, but it wasn't so difficult. I was very lucky the way I got into Sunderland. I was a big, massive Sunderland supporter at the time, and I had broken my arm at school playing football. I was about 10 or 11 years old. I was at home, I couldn't go to school and my dad said: 'What's wrong?' And I said: "Oh, I'm miserable, I'm missing my Football." He said he would take the day off work and we would go and see Sunderland train. I hadn't seen them before. I'd been to a couple of games, but never seen any of them close up. So we went through to Cleadon where they trained and there were three pitches.There was nobody else there, just me and my father, so we stood and watched them train.
I was in awe, just watching them train. There was Colin Todd, Charlie Hurley, Monty (Jim Montgomery), Jimmy McNeil, Jim Baxter - all these great players. And there was me, this little, scruffy kid from Annfield Plain - glasses, ginger hair, a little overcoat and little trainers. Just basic clothing, that's all the kids wore back then.We got so wet and drenched and at the end of the training session, they came off. As we were walking off I

was mixing in and that, walking off with them and amongst them, looking at them, because they were all giants to me. And there was a guy there called Cecil Irwin, who was a right-back in the first team. He was walking off next to me and he saw my arm and asked what I had been doing. I told him I had broken my arm playing football and he asked me if I was a footballer and where I had come from. He asked me what I was doing there and I told him I was from Annfield Plain and just came along to watch them train because I love Sunderland. He told us to follow the team bus and come back to the stadium and he would show us around the dressing rooms and the pitch.

I was speechless. I'd been to the ground, I'd stood in the crowd with everybody else, but to be able to get the chance to get on the pitch and that!

So me and my dad followed him. Then we waited about 45 minutes and Cecil, true to his word, took me into the dressing room with all the other lads. I was pretty embarrassed as a few of them didn't have any clothes on and they were a bit bigger than me (laughs).

Then he took us onto the pitch. I was in awe. I wanted to play, that's all I ever wanted to do, and I'd gone on there and I knew that's all I wanted to do. So he took me back in and we were walking round, and I know it sounds strange, but we were walking past the chief scout's office and the chief scout - a little Scottish guy called Charlie Ferguson - came out.

He asked Cec who I was and I told him I played for Stanley Boys. He said: 'You're not Micky Horswill are you?' This was the chief scout of Sunderland! He'd been told of a ginger kid who played for Stanley Boys that he had to go and see, he told me. I couldn't believe he said my name before I told him who I was. It was such a buzz I just wanted to explode.

He said he'd had letters and knew all about me and was going to come and see me play. He told me to give him a ring when I got fit and had my plaster off and he would come and watch me play. After that I was out training and running and kicking the

ball against the wall and everything.
I didn't want to phone him until I had played a few games. I
went to a game and I was playing for the school and I saw him.
He asked me if I would come through every Tuesday and
Thursday night after school and train with the juniors. So every
Tuesday and Thursday for about six years, I travelled from
Stanley to Sunderland on the bus.
 In that five or six years I must have missed only about four or
five sessions. I was just so enthusiastic, determined and
disciplined to do it. That's all
I did. That was my life for all of school.

BERNIE

You played in the 1973 FA Cup Final as a 19-year-old against
Leeds United at Wembley and Sunderland won 1-0. Could you
believe at such a tender age you were playing in a major cup
final for your home town club?

MICK

It was crazy. We got draws in the last few moments against
Reading and Notts County in the first and second rounds and
brought them back to Roker Park. We never thought of winning
the cup - we were in the lower half of the Second Division and a
Second Division team never wins it. We knew we had the basis
of a good side, but we still weren't doing well in the league.
None of us had played at a First Division stadium and we
wanted to see what it was like to play one of the big names.I was
a little bit late for training on the day of the third round draw and
heard a big, massive roar as I was running in. We got Man City
away and at the time they were bigger than Man United, one of
the biggest clubs in the country. They had Mike Summerbee,
Colin Bell, Francis Lee, Dennis Law, Rodney Marsh.
They had a fantastic team. It was the biggest crowd any of us

had played in front of at Man City. Tony Towers was playing for them. He was a bit of a hothead and midway through the second half he got sent off for giving me the Glasgow kiss. We were 2-1 up and we got an equaliser - I scored actually - and brought them back to Sunderland in front of a full house of 60,000. It's been voted the best game at Sunderland over the century. We beat them 3-1 and played fantastic and that was the first time we thought we could do something. That put us into the quarter-finals and we thought we had a big chance if we got a home draw, because there was still quite a few Second Division sides in the competition.

We drew Luton Town at home. They were below us in the Second Division and we beat them 2-0 at Roker Park. There used to be about 15,000 people camping out on a Saturday night around Roker Park to get the tickets for the next home game, to make sure they got a token for the next cup game coming up. It was unbelievable. We beat the famous Arsenal in the semi-finals to book a date in the final with Leeds, who were one of the biggest league sides in the world. We didn't expect to win, but we knew we had a very good chance with the team that we had, because we had a great balance. Monty was a top goalkeeper, our back four - Dick Malone, Dave Watson, Ritchie Pitt and Ron Guthrie - were all big, strong guys that nothing could beat them in the air. We played 4-3-3 every game and our middle three were Bobby Kerr, who was a little general, on the right, I was in the centre and Ian Porterfield, the footballer in the team, was on the left. I couldn't play but I used to win the ball and give it to Ian or Bobby. We had a big striker who we could hit in Vic Halom, and Dennis Tueart and Billy Hughes around him. They were very quick and good finishers and were at home on the wing or in the middle, so they floated about. So we had that balance, everyone played for each other, and we had a settled team. None of us were nervous for the final, we were so relaxed. We just wanted to go and play against them. It was a fantastic atmosphere at Wembley, as you can imagine. It was just a dream and the only time I got nervous was when we came out of the tunnel. We were stood facing the Leeds guys during the national anthem and they were looking at you, steam coming out of them. But when the national anthem finished and the game started it was fantastic. The game went so smooth for us.

BERNIE

Bob Stokoe was your manager. What was he like?

MICK

He was a strange guy. The first time he came in was a Friday afternoon. The other manager Alan Brown, who was my favourite manager, had been sacked. As I said, we weren't doing very well when Bob Stokoe came in. He sat the first team down and told us he was a Newcastle supporter and how much he loved the club after playing for them in the FA Cup. But he promised that while he was in charge he would give 100% effort and all his time to get us where we wanted to be. He did that to be fair and for his first game in charge he played the same team from the week before because he hadn't had much time to work with us. He came into the dressing room and we were all stripped. He didn't say very much but he came in with a bottle of whisky, took the top off and put it on the physio table in the middle of the dressing room. He told all of us to have a swig before we went out. We thought he was off his head - a black and white who was trying to get us drunk before we played! But everybody that went out had a big swig - Billy Hughes drank about half the bottle! It was just one of his ways to get us all together.

BERNIE

Was he a strict disciplinarian?

MICK

He tried to be. He brought in Arthur Cox and Arthur was a disciplinarian. He was like the sergeant major and Bob was the guy who was caring and gentle and tried to put his arm around you. But if something went wrong, he could raise his fist and that. But Arthur was the one that tried to be the sergeant major of the two of them.

BERNIE

What's the story about the teeth?

MICK

We had four guys in the team who had no teeth or didn't have many - Ritchie Pitt, Bobby Kerr, Vic Halom and Billy Hughes. So during games they used to put their false teeth in their pockets. But in the FA Cup Final we were going to do a lap of honour whether we won or lost. The lads were stressing about meeting royalty and being on television with no teeth in. So we came up with an idea to get little velvet boxes and put their teeth in. Joe Bolton, who was my room mate at the time, and the physio Johnny Ward would look after two each and bring them out. It was mayhem after the game when we won - everybody was running everywhere and cuddling everybody so much that it took us ages to get together and go up to get our medals. It was all timed in those days. You had to line up, walk up the steps in single file and get your medal and we went way over the time. There was a few of us that had assembled at the bottom of the stairs. Bobby Kerr, the captain who was supposed to be at the front, was missing. The steward was going absolutely mental because he couldn't get us together to go up. The royalty were waiting to give us our medals and that.

What had happened was the guys couldn't find Joe and Johnny because there was millions of people on the pitch and they couldn't find the guys with the boxes to get the teeth. So they were running round the pitch looking for Joe and Johnny to get the boxes with their teeth in before they went up to get their medals. We told the steward that the lads were looking for their teeth and he said: "We're giving you medals. not pork pies. 'Go get them and get up and get your medals!' (Laughs)

BERNIE

Ian Porterfield, the man that scored the all important goal that day, has sadly passed away. What are your memories of him?

MICK

God bless him. When I first got into the first team, I used to play centre back and after a few games the boss put me in midfield, because I had so much energy. I wanted to do everything, so he put me in midfield and we called Ian 'The General'. He was a lovely footballer, similar to Jim Baxter. He took me aside, because he was one of the senior players, and gave me a pep talk. He said I'd got into the team because I warranted it and he told me to win the ball, not to elaborate and to keep it simple. He said that way I would stay in the team and have a great career. He used to take me to a little café in the centre of Washington every lunch time and all he wanted to do was talk football. He was the only one out of the team who went on to become a manager and when I think about it that's probably his background for going into management. Because the rest of us players didn't want to talk about the last game and the next game coming up, we just wanted to talk about drinking and birds. He just loved football and he went on to have a great career. He went to Chelsea and finished over in Korea. He had a really good career and he was a great player as well. God bless him.

BERNIE

When you returned to Annfield Plain in Durham to your mother's house, you took the FA Cup trophy to show her and I believe it went missing?

MICK

In them days, we didn't know, but when we won the cup it came back to Sunderland with us, at the ground. If you wanted to take the cup to a function or something, you just went and asked. So you used to go and get the cup - it was in a big wooden box - and take it to wherever you wanted and bring it back the next day, or two days later, or whatever. So my dad suggested that I bring it back home - I lived in a little council house on Annfield Plain - and we would get some photos taken with it with the neighbours. The neighbours loved me to bits, winning the FA Cup. I brought it home and there must have been two or three hundred people queuing outside the house for their pictures with the cup.The house was absolutely packed, people were coming in all day. I went for a cup of tea and when I came back in to see what was going on and the cup wasn't there. I asked my mam where it was and she told me someone must have borrowed it. I said: 'You can't borrow the FA Cup!'
Someone had taken it to their house in the middle of the estate and the FA Cup was being walked around with people getting their photos taken with it. They brought it back, there was no hassle with it. But I was just a little bit worried at the time because I didn't know where it was!

BERNIE

After 98 games for Sunderland you were transferred to Man
City. Did that come as a shock?

MICK

It came as a massive shock.
I didn't get on with Stokoe very well, and after the FA Cup he
didn't really fancy me. We used to have fights and everything
and after one Saturday game he said he didn't want me to come
to the ground for training the next day. He told me to come to
the ground at 1pm, so I did. When I got there, there was about
50 or 60 press men in the car park. They asked what was going
on with me and I said I didn't know and asked them if they
could tell me. They told me they thought I was on my way,
which I didn't think was possible because nobody had
mentioned it. Remember I was just a young kid - I was only 20
and didn't know anything about transfers.
So I went into the ground and somebody said the manager was
waiting up in the directors room with Dennis Tueart. I thought
we were in trouble for going out clubbing or something, because
we used to go out a lot.
The boss was there with the chairman and they told me they had
brought me in because they wanted me to go to Ramside Hall at
4pm the same day. I thought it was strange, so I drove to
Ramside Hall and the chairman was there in his Rolls Royce.
Me and Dennis sat in the back with the boss and chairman in
the front and we set off down the A1. Nobody spoke all the way
until we got to Wetherby and the chairman suggested we go into
the Wetherby Hotel for a cup of coffee. When we got there,
Tony Towers - the guy who nutted me and got sent off in the cup
- was in reception with Tony Book. I pointed Towers out to
Dennis and told him we should do him over! (laughs) The
chairman finally said it was Manchester City that wanted to buy

me. They had come down to meet us on a Sunday afternoon and we couldn't believe it because they were a massive club. We got introduced to Ron Saunders and he arranged fees and things. Me and Tony Towers were going to swap clubs. It was a Sunday night and Saunders said: 'If you want to play for Manchester City, be at the training ground tomorrow at 10am.'

It was the same thing for Dennis. So I went home and told me mam and dad what was happening and that I was going to have to leave home if I wanted to go, which I'd never done before. I was crying my eyes out and I thought about it all night. I rang Dennis at 4am and we both said we were going to go to Manchester. So we went down and trained around the stadium at Maine Road and we signed late on in the afternoon. That was on the Monday and we made our debuts at home to Man United in front of 50-60,000 on the Wednesday. I played in midfield and the forward line that played in front of me was: Summerbee, Bell, Lee, Dennis Law and Rodney Marsh. It was mind blowing. They were my superstars that I had grown up watching and wanting to be one of them and here I was, playing in behind them, just having to win the ball for them and give them it.

It was just a weird, weird feeling, but they took me under their wing and I became really good friends with Rodney Marsh.

BERNIE

During your stint in Manchester, I believe you struck up a partnership outside of football with the late, great George Best. There must be some great stories. Is it true you were the doorman?

MICK

(Laughs) Doorman was the best job in the world, I'll tell you. There used to be bunny girls coming round at four in the morning and all kinds. Miss Worlds and everything, it was unbelievable. He retired that year when I met him and he became a really good friend. He still wanted to play football, he just didn't want all the hassle of the football club. Every Wednesday night, we used to drive about 20 miles to a place called Stanley Bridge, where there was a league that played on a Wednesday. We hired one court and there was Rodney and myself, Besty, Wilf McGuinness - the former manager of Man United - and a guy called Geoff Baker, who was a big friend of ours who played in goal. The teams that used to come and play in the league on the other pitch used to play us for five or 10 minutes as a warm-up and they thought it was fantastic. Anyway, Besty took me out on my 21st birthday one night after football and said we would stop and have a drink at every pub we pass and get back on the road again. There must have been 40 or 50 pubs all the way back to Manchester and we didn't miss one. Then we got to Besty's pub and he said everyone was to have a drink from every optic, bottle and pump in the bar. Then we went to his nightclub and we drank five crates of champagne. He had the biggest party and we were in there for about three days. I missed training. I mean, he was great to know, he was my best friend and I'd do it all again, but he knackered my career up.

I was a budding international, a young kid coming through. I'd just got into the England squad with Don Revie. He put me in his squad because he knew about our FA Cup run and playing against his team. The World Cup was two years away but with George my career went and I stopped playing and everything for a good few years. It just knackered my career up for a while.

As I say, knowing the people I have known and met, I would do it all again, no bother, no problem at all.

BERNIE

You departed Manchester and ended up at Plymouth Argyle.
Why Plymouth?

MICK

It wasn't really a popular club. At the time we were one of the
top clubs in the First Division and they had just got promoted to
the Second Division. But when I first started playing for
Sunderland, the first guy who took me on as an apprentice, made
me a professional and gave me my debut, was Alan Brown.
Plymouth had a young manager called Tony Waiters, who was a
goalkeeper who played for England and Blackpool. He asked
Alan Brown to go and give him a hand and provide some
experience and that's where Cloughie learned all his business
from Alan Brown. They needed a player who could help sort
the team out and Alan phoned me that night and the next day I
was on the train down there. That's why I went to Plymouth.

BERNIE

You spent three or four years at Hull City after Plymouth. Did
you enjoy it?

MICK

That was strange, because I hadn't drunk for a while and Hull
City had a big drinking team. We had Billy Whitehurst and all
the guys, we had Steve McClaren. We had a really good but
hectic team and I started drinking again. We used to go all over
the place and everyone was frightened to death of us outside of
football as well because of big Billy. I remember once when we
went on pre-season tour to Holland - and this is one of the
reasons I stopped drinking. I was like the assistant manager and

captain of the team. We went on the ferry and I can't remember anything about the trip because we all got gassed. We went out the first night there and played a bit of a game, without a problem. We went out on the town afterwards me and Billy but I had to go to bed as soon as we got back to the hotel because I had no cohesion. I remember waking up in bed thirsty and hearing music in this big, massive hotel.

I thought I was missing out on something, so I got up and walked into this big reception hall into a disco. I walked through everybody on the dance floor straight to the bar and got a drink. A few of the lads came over and asked me what I was doing and I said I'd got up to have a drink because I thought I was missing something. It was then that they politely pointed out that I had no clothes on!

I had nothing on but I was that far gone I didn't realise.

I'd walked through hundreds of people with nothing on and that's one of the reasons I packed in.

Sixteen years and I've never had a drink.

BERNIE

Your career finished at 29 due to injury. What was the injury and how difficult was that to take?

MICK

It was a nightmare. I tore an Achilles tendon while at Hull City and for two seasons I tried to get fit. I had operations in London as well and I did come round and started playing a little bit. But because my Achilles wasn't working properly, every time that I trained my calf would take all the strain and it used to explode and that was me out for four to six weeks.

But on one of the occasions my calf didn't explode there was some Chinese guys there who had come over to get players for their team in Hong Kong. They flew into London on a Tuesday and the only game that night was Hull City against Scunthorpe, so they flew up to watch it. They asked to see me, Billy Whitehurst and a guy called Nick Deacy, who used to play for Wales, after the game. Eventually they offered us good money to go over. My calf had exploded in that game and I had to get carried off. So I thought my career was finished and I might as well go over for a good holiday, get paid for two or three years just for having a holiday. So they met us in Manchester two or three days later. Billy and Nick decided not to go, but I decided still to go, just to get out of the way.

BERNIE

The team was Happy Valley.

MICK

I played for Happy Valley with Bobby Moore, Alan Ball, Tommy Hutchinson. Tony Pulis, the Stoke City manager, played and Besty came over to visit me three or four times. One of the wealthiest women in Hong Kong asked him to play for her team and offered him £15,000 to play one game in 1980. He played one game and did okay and she asked him to play again, so he asked for £30,000. She said it was okay but he would have to go to the Philippines for a holiday and do some training.
He said he wanted paying again if he had to train and asked for a Rolls Royce sending to England.
She thought about it for two days and refused, but he got £45,000 for two games. He didn't play 20 minutes, the second game.

BERNIE

Was money the attraction of the move?

MICK

No, it was never massive money. We were never going to be
millionaires. We got about 300, 400 quid a week. But I went
because my career had finished and I always wanted to see Asia.
Getting paid for it as well, that was the attraction to go.

BERNIE

While in Hong Kong, you came out of a nightclub in the early
hours of the morning and jumped in a taxi with two uninvited
guests. Tell me about that again.

MICK

We went out there and stopped with a couple of mates of mine.
Besty used to get all the good looking girls, always did, you
know what he was like. So one night we went out, we were
flying to the Philippines the next day
for a holiday, the two of us, at 8am. I woke up mortled drunk in
a nightclub at 1am after being out all day, not knowing where
we were. I looked along and Mooro was asleep next to me and
Besty and Tony were asleep on the bar. So I nudged them and
said we had better go and get our bags for flying. He told me he
would get them and I stayed and had a drink with Mooro before
I decided I had to get out of there. I remember crawling up the
steps on my hands and knees to get out of the nightclub. I got to
the top and it was red hot, as you can imagine in Hong Kong,
and when the heat hit me it made me feel really ill.
So I flagged a big yellow taxi down and just as I was getting in
the back somebody pushed me from behind. I thought I was

getting mugged but when I turned round it was two beautiful Chinese girls who had obviously been having a good time. They were immaculately dressed and got in the cab. One had a long ginger wig and the other had white hair, which also looked like a wig. I told the driver where I was staying and we hadn't gone three minutes into the journey and they nearly had all my clothes off. I was just lying there like the king and the driver had one eye on us and one eye on the road. They did all kinds to me and I thought it was heaven.

When we got to Tony's house 20 minutes later I paid the driver and got out carrying all my clothes and the two girls - who didn't speak a word of English - got out as well. I was thinking they were two darlings and Besty would be over the moon. When he opened the door I told him they were incredible and would just get stuck into him. I flopped onto the couch still mortled drunk and the blonde one started messing around with my Niagaras. So he lifted the ginger one up and ran into the bedroom. But just as I was nodding off Besty came running in. He said: 'Horswill you bastard, it's two f****** blokes!' I looked down and the blonde was still on my Niagaras. So we gave them a mouthful, and it was so funny it was two blokes. I've still got their phone numbers if you want them.

BERNIE

When you returned to England you fell out of love with football and didn't go to a game for 10 years. Why?

MICK

I didn't fall out of love with football, I still loved football. But I was so upset because I was at my fittest. I was a really, really fit bloke and a fantastic runner.

That's how I did my Achilles, running to train for marathons and things. So I was so upset that I couldn't play any more that couldn't go and watch it.

So I never went to watch a game for nearly 10 years and never went anywhere near one. I used to watch a little bit on television from one eye and make out I wasn't watching. But I used to hate watching it because I wasn't involved any more. It was a nightmare for me.

BERNIE

You got the opportunity to join Century's - now Real Radio's - Legends show between six and eight every night alongside myself and Malcolm. How have you found it?

MICK

It's been fantastic. I took over from Eric Gates, who was fantastic on the show. Everybody I'd spoken to said that he was really good and he was good. Whatever's gone on has gone on and he's left, but I spoke to him before I came on the show and told him that Century had approached me for a few interviews for the job. He said it was good on me if I got and that it was a great job and I'd enjoy it if I got it. So that eased me a little bit. I came and because I get on so well with the two of you I've really enjoyed it, we've had a good laugh. It's not like a standard radio show, we come on and speak our minds and just have a laugh and we enjoy ourselves. It's not the norm, which is what I enjoy.

BERNIE

You are also part of the former Sunderland players' committee. What does that job entail and who is involved?

MICK

We have got about 80 former players who pay £25 to become a member of our society. There are six of us on the committee - Dick Malone, Jim Montgomery, Gary Bennett, a guy called Winston who used to be the secretary for Sunderland quite a while ago, and Jimmy Shoulder who used to play in the 60s. We organise dinners, golf days, charity do's for kiddies.
We have got lots of members who if we have a function or a golf day all the people come and play for us. They get a footballer to play in their team and the money we make for that doesn't come to our society, it goes to the kiddies in our local area. This year its been for Zoe's Place and things like that and Tilly, who had a little baby who lost her arms because she had meningitis. So it's for causes like that.

BERNIE

Over the last few years Sunderland have been transformed. Would you agree?

MICK

It has been fantastic.
Just before Niall Quinn came, we had a chairman in Bob Murray who didn't want anything to do with former players. He just didn't see that as anything to do with the club or of benefit to the club. So we had to buy tickets if we wanted to go to the game, things like that. You weren't invited in. Quinny came and he's completely the opposite. He can't get enough of the former players. He can see the value of ex-team players like myself, Jim Montgomery, Dick Malone, the cup team, and people like that. Gary Bennett walks about the place and people see us thinking it's a great friendly club. They can come up and talk to the former players,

and that's far better than being in the   background and not being able to talk to people. You want to be among the people. When I go to games I go and sit in the crowd because I think it's better than sitting with the sandwich brigade upstairs, and Quinny's taken that on board.

He has us going into different boxes, he has us going to dinners for him,he has us doing all kinds of things. He is just fantastic.Every former player who wants to go and see any game is allowed two free tickets. I think that's fantastic.

BERNIE

What about manager Roy Keane?

MICK

Roy is a strange guy. I've met him a couple of times.
We have a football game once a year to raise funds for charity.
It's ex-players, our committee and our consortium they come over from Ireland and play against us. I think you played in it last year and Roy was there. He's a strange guy, a loner I think. He doesn't want to mix. You don't see him out and about very much. He doesn't like talking to many people, so he's a bit of a strange guy. Don't get me wrong, he's done a fantastic job. When he came we were bottom of the Championship and he got us promotion in his first year. He has kept us in the Premier League for two seasons, so you can't grumble at what he has done. He has made a lot of mistakes, he admits that himself. And even though he has made those mistakes we are still in the Premier League. This year we have got a much better standard of players, and I think a far better team than we had last year, so hopefully we can keep growing and building on that and get up to where Middlesbrough are. They have been there for 15 years. To be established, to be there for 10 or 15 years without getting relegated, that's the goal.

BERNIE

What was your best football moment?

MICK

Probably my debut.

BERNIE

Overriding the FA Cup Final?

MICK

All I wanted to do was be a footballer and to go out and play for the first time was fantastic. It was at Preston North End, who were managed by Nobby Stiles at the time, on a horrible Tuesday night. I used to carry the skips into the dressing room and put all of the gear out. Alan Brown, who I went to Plymouth for, was our manager and at about 6pm he said he wanted to see me in the passage. He said I'd done well for him and he wanted me to play sweeper that night and show what I could do.
He said: 'Your father's not here, so I'm your father now.
'I'm giving you your chance, prove me right and get out there and show me what you can do.'
From that moment it was just a fantastic feeling. We won 3-1.

BERNIE

Your worst moment?

MICK

My injury, when I did my Achilles. I always believed I'd be back fit again. But the day I had to say I wasn't playing was the worst moment of my career.

BERNIE

Where did the nickname 'Tiddler' come from?

MICK

It just came up lately, I don't know where it came from. Somebody called Bernie Slaven just christened me 'The Tiddler'.

BERNIE

And it stuck

HONOURS

MICHAEL FREDERICK HORSWILL

PLAYING CAREER HISTORY

1971-1974 Sunderland
1974-1975 Man City
1975-1978 Plymouth Argyle
1978-1982 Hull City
1982-1983 Happy Valley

PLAYING CAREER HONOURS(winners)

Sunderland

1973 FA Cup.

Micky with the late great George Best.

FA Cup win

"They shot the wrong Kennedy in 63."

What bob paisley told Alan

ALAN KENNEDY
SUNDERLAND

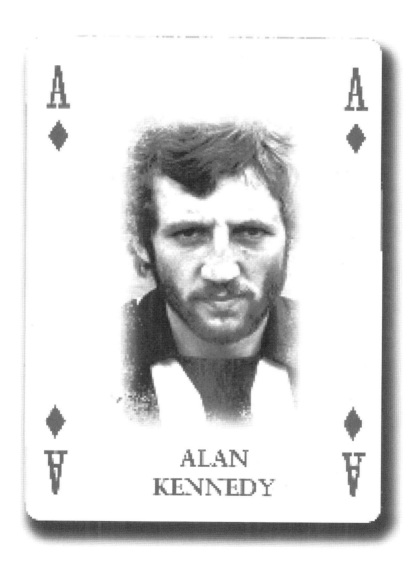

Alan Philip Kennedy was born on August 31, 1954 in Sunderland. Despite his birthplace, he came through the ranks at Newcastle United. His debut for the Magpies arrived against Stoke City in March 1973.

Alan was very seldom injured. He was a good, strong defender who loved to drive forward and he scored some glorious and important goals.

I met Barney - as he's known - while working for Real Radio. I work up here in the North East on the Three Legends and Alan worked in Manchester along with Graeme Sharp, Mickey Thomas and Gary Owen on a similar show. I played against him both when he was at Sunderland and in the Masters football and have always found him friendly, fun-loving and genuine.

I interviewed Alan over the phone - I was afraid to travel to Liverpool to meet up with him in case my car got nicked!

BERNIE

Where were you born?

ALAN

I was born in Kale Road in Sunderland. My mother was from Hetton-le-Hole,
which is Bob Paisley country, and my father was from the Newcastle area. I was brought up in a little pit village called Shiney Row. We lived there quite a while, then we moved to Penshaw, next to the monument.

BERNIE

Was that the posh end?

ALAN

Yes, it was the posh end. It was still a council house but we decided to go there and we never looked back. The council were not very happy, but we sold it and got a few bob for it! It was a great upbringing because I used to absolutely love playing football. Penshaw is on a hill. Kicking uphill was a bit traumatic, but going downhill was great, we used to love it. It was 25-a-side usually!

BERNIE

Who did you support as a kid? Were you a Sunderland fan?

ALAN

Yes, I was. My mother's family persuaded me to support Sunderland. My favourite players were George Mulhall and Nick Sharkey, and Jim Montgomery was the best goalkeeper I had ever seen. But my favourite player of all was a guy called Charlie Hurley. He was a wonderful centre half - big, imposing and stood his ground. I used to look up to him and wish I could play like him. Eventually I probably did, but in a different position. My father loved Newcastle, so I was torn between two teams - the red and whites and the black and whites.
I was eventually persuaded around the age of 10 or 11 that Newcastle were the better team, because my brother signed to play in the youth team. I eventually went for a trial and they

thought I was half decent. I think the only reason I got in the team was that I kicked the ball with my left foot!

BERNIE

There's not many of them left.

ALAN

Classy ones, you're right.

BERNIE

Which Newcastle manager signed you?

ALAN

It was Joe Harvey, who was brilliant. Once when I was injured in the olden days, I remember going in and I had to wait outside while a greyhound went in to get some treatment!
It was a fantastic upbringing, there were some real greats of the time there. Bob Moncur scored a couple of goals in a European Cup final against Ujpest Dozsa and I used to look up to players like that. Wyn Davies was a hero of mine back in the late 1960s with his aerial power, and Bryan 'Pop' Robson scored goals for fun. At that stage of my career I was more of a striker than a defender. I used to play outside left as a kid in my school team and scored quite a few goals. Again, the reason I got in the team was because I could give a bit of balance to the team on the left-hand side.

BERNIE

Being a Sunderland fan, were you in two minds about joining Newcastle or didn't it bother you?

ALAN

No. My brother Keith, who was there before me and two-and-a-half years older, advised me to take the deal they were offering But at that time I wasn't so sure that I wanted to become a footballer. My dad told me to stay on at school and get my qualifications just in case I didn't make it as a player. So in the end I went to the old Washington Grammar School. I was there for an extra year and managed to get all the qualifications I could. Then Newcastle came along and asked if I would like to sign an apprenticeship. Normally you get a two-year contract, but they told me that I could only have the one year as I was coming up to 17 and they felt one year would be enough, and obviously it was. I made my debut in 1973 against Stoke City. The problem was that my brother was a left-back as well.
I was asked to play at right-back in a reserve game. They said it would be good experience but I was like a fish out of water. Everything was coming onto my left foot. In the end one of us had to move on and eventually it was Keith. He didn't have the best time in a first team team game against Nottingham Forest and they decided to sell him to Bury. He played there for the next 11 years so he had a great career, just not so good at Newcastle. I took his place and I don't know if he has ever forgiven me.

BERNIE

What were your highlights at St James'?

ALAN

It was a big learning curve. Joe resigned after the 1974 cup final, then Keith Burkinshaw was there and a lad called Dave Smith. They were great coaches and I really enjoyed working with them, and then Gordon Lee came in.

BERNIE

What was he like?

ALAN

I didn't think at the time that he really knew much about the football world. You had to have a little bit of experience and knowledge about the game and he had come in at the lower end and found himself at Newcastle because they wanted him at that particular time. He tried to keep things ticking over but I have to say he infuriated two or three players.

BERNIE

He got rid of Malcolm Macdonald.

ALAN

He did and Malcolm wasn't happy with him. Gordon Lee didn't think he worked enough for the team. But Malcolm had his attributes - speed and scoring goals - and he was a very strong player. Terry Hibbitt was another one that had a problem, so in the end Terry and Malcolm left the club and one or two others did as well. He brought in his own men and then all of a sudden left to take over at Everton. Richard Dinnis then took over. In 1977 player power was a big thing and a few of us stood up for him as assistant manager and got him the job.
He got the sack after a bad run of 10 games and that was when Bill McGarry came in and decided enough was enough.

But I really did enjoy it under Joe Harvey. He was one of those managers who would allow you to go out and express yourself. Although he was a bit of a smoker we didn't particularly mind that. But I suppose he was a bit overrun by the player power at Newcastle at the time and certainly Malcolm Macdonald and Terry Hibbitt were two that voiced their opinions.

BERNIE

Did you sit in the background?

ALAN

I sat in the background because I was a young lad. I was just coming through. I wasn't a shop steward in those days, I was one of those who listened to the manager and chairman. But there always seemed to be a problem at the club and player power was quickly quashed in 1977 when Bill McGarry arrived. We were a good cup team at that time. In those six years I was there we reached the 1974 FA Cup final and the 1976 League Cup final. Although the fans loved going to Wembley we felt we could get a steady position in the league. But I suppose that didn't materialise because we were one of those teams that would go out there and try and win 4-3 rather than 1-0. Looking back I thought we had strong full-backs with me on the left and Irving Nattrass on the right. I felt if we could get it right in the middle, and certainly Bob Moncur was there for a little while and Pat Howard and people like that, we had a chance.
Then it seemed to go haywire and we conceded an awful lot of goals which was not the right grounding for getting higher up the league.

BERNIE

How would you describe your playing style?

ALAN

I wasn't one of those players that adapted quickly to my position. I always felt that I was more of a forward than a defensive player. It was only when I joined Liverpool that I remembered I had to defend as well, but I always wanted to get forward. People like Tommy Craig and Terry Hibbitt encouraged me to get forward and they would cover me.

I was probably as quick as anybody in those days. Although I wasn't the tallest of players, I was brave as well and sometimes a bit daft and a bit foolhardy. I wasn't one of the best players and one of the things I did miss out on was playing for my country. I got picked in 1974 to represent England, but I had a serious knee ligament operation and unfortunately I couldn't play for Newcastle or my country so I was very disappointed with that.

It took 10 years for me to eventually get back in the England squad and I made my debut in 1984. When I started all I wanted to do was play for Newcastle. Try and play in every game and when I got injured I wanted to be back as soon as possible. I think I always showed a good attitude to everything and wanted to win at everything, even if it was five-a-side.

I wasn't blessed with great ability but I had a big heart. I would fight anybody on the pitch for Newcastle at the time because that was my team.

BERNIE

You joined Liverpool via a phone box didn't you?

ALAN

That's exactly how it happened. There were no agents in those days and local reporter Bob Cass got to know about it.

He came knocking on my door telling me to give Liverpool a ring because they wanted to sign me. We weren't actually on the phone, so I went down to the one and only phone box at Bramwell shops and rang Liverpool. I got through to the club secretary Peter Robinson, who confirmed their interest, and the deal was done after Liverpool initially offered £300,000, which was still a lot of money in those days. Bill McGarry came to me after it was all settled and said that I didn't have to go and Newcastle would give me a bit of a rise. I didn't want to leave but Liverpool had just won the European Cup and I had to set my stall out. Leeds were also interested and had put in a package for me and Irving Nattrass to go there. But of course I went to Liverpool. I'd asked my dad for advice about it because it was after my mother had just died and he said whatever decision I made it would be the wrong one!

He said: "Listen son, if you stay with us you'll regret not joining the European champions. "But if you go and join Liverpool, you'll think you should be looking after your dad and sister as you've just lost your mother."

So it was a difficult decision. I wanted him to say 'go' or 'stay', it wasn't the answer I was looking for. But I made my mind up fairly quickly and then I went. When I arrived Peter Robinson was telling me all about the club and what they achieved and asked me if I would like to join the players in a five-a-side game. I was replacing Joey Jones but I was that bad in the five-a-side game they said: "Come back Joey Jones!" I had the nerve to say to Liverpool that I wanted to go home and have a word about the move with my dad. I did, he eventually said I might as well sign and the rest is history.

BERNIE

You played with players like Kenny Dalglish, Alan Hansen and Graeme Souness. Did you feel intimidated when you first arrived at Anfield?

ALAN

Yes, I did feel intimidated. I felt as though I knew a couple of the players with England - Phil Thompson, Terry McDermott and David Fairclough. I knew what kind of players the others were. Dalglish had scored in the 1978 European Cup final, Hansen was developing into the player that he was and I had played against Souness at Newcastle.
The local lads Sammy Lee and Jimmy Case were absolutely fantastic and made me feel so welcome. And although I lived in a city centre hotel for a while I felt every moment at the club was great. I wasn't first choice full-back because they had Emlyn Hughes there and Joey Jones and as I made my debut I was told I would be under pressure for my place.

BERNIE

Being brought up in Glasgow as a Celtic fan, Dalglish was my hero. How good was he and what was he like as a character?

ALAN

He was a very easy person to get on with and he was one of those players that everybody looked up to because he had exceptional skill, both in the midfield and as a forward. He took a lot of bumps and bruises and he put himself in areas that other players wouldn't go. But I think all in all if you look back on the whole team, anybody could actually play in it and get away with it, even if you weren't the biggest or brightest player. Kenny certainly lifted everyone's spirits. It would be difficult to separate him, Souness and Hansen as to who is the greatest player because they all contributed to Liverpool's success in that period. I was just a left-back who had just come into the team and never wanted to be out of it, but competition from other players meant that I didn't play all the games.

Kenny was, and probably still is, one of the greatest players - if not the greatest player - to pull on the red shirt of Liverpool.

BERNIE

What was Bob Paisley like as a manager? He came across as an elderly gentleman who was a bit of a mumbler.

ALAN

He didn't like the media side of things and didn't cope with going on television. If he was around in today's game, he would probably pass it on to someone else. He never liked communicating and was a shy man really who loved his football and family. He let the players do the talking on the pitch and even in the team meetings, he wasn't good at demonstrating as a manager should have been. He told us to learn the Liverpool way, work hard, make things happen and defend as a team. There wasn't any special introductions for any particular game. I remember Don Revie having a dossier on the opposition. We spent about three minutes on a Friday morning talking about the opposition. No disrespect to them, but I'm sure the opposition spent 20 minutes talking about us. We were European champions and league champions in 1978 with a record number of points. Heaven forbid if we lost a couple of games. Bob would go absolutely berserk and would have a go at the captain,

Phil Thompson or Graeme Souness, telling them he wasn't having it and to get it sorted. We would have a couple of nights out but we were all business when we had to be.

I remember playing a game at your old club Middlesbrough when we opened up a shop on the afternoon and ended up having a couple of beers. Middlesbrough were playing reasonable football in those days and we ended up drawing 0-0. But you were made aware that if you let the club down you would be out and I was glad to last seven years there.

BERNIE

No doubt you have answered this a million times, but could you believe you scored the winner in the 1981 European Cup final against Real Madrid in Paris? That Liverpool side had Ian Rush and Dalglish in it, and it was Alan Kennedy who scored the winner.

ALAN

Well, I couldn't at the time because my job was to basically defend. Obviously after 80-odd minutes of the game it was 0-0. A rush of blood came to my head to get forward and I certainly didn't expect Ray Kennedy to throw the ball to me. I was sort of turning to make a bit of space for people like Souness or Sammy Lee to get the ball or maybe have a cross-shot or whatever. It was totally unexpected when he threw the ball. I chested it down, carried it to the box and eventually the goalkeeper made the final move of going to his left expecting the cross and the ball went in at the near post. If he had stayed there I'd have got a right rollocking from the manager because the goalkeeper would have collected it and kicked it up field.

I was waiting for the whistle thinking there might have been an infringement or something. It didn't come and I ran off celebrating and the fans were trying to get on the pitch. If there had been gates I would have run through them into Paris! David Johnson came over and tried to push me in the moat between the pitch and the fans! I asked him what he was doing and he asked if I had meant to score the way it happened.

I said: "Of course I did!"

BERNIE

Did you mean it?

ALAN

It was one of those decisions. If I crossed the ball I'd have got a rollocking for not having a go. I was nine yards from goal, you've got to have a go. The ball could have gone anywhere because it wasn't a great pitch, but fortunately it went in the back of the net and it obviously won the game for Liverpool.

BERNIE

It must have been some night in Paris!

ALAN

It was a great night. The lads went out and took the cup with them and it came back about half five in the morning.
Phil Thompson and I took it out the next day and got our pictures taken. We took it onto the plane and then Phil took it to his local pub in Kirkby for people to get their photos taken with it. Phil got so drunk he forgot about it and left it in there! He got a phone call the next morning from Peter Robinson asking where the cup was and Phil said it was next to him. It wasn't, it was still in the bar at the pub! It's amazing the things you get up to with the European Cup!

BERNIE

I'd never know! You lifted the European Cup yet again in a penalty shoot out against Roma in 1984. You scored one of the penalties - what are your memories of that?

ALAN

Bruce Grobbelaar was brilliant on that particular day. I didn't realise what he was doing when he was putting their players off. The game finished 1-1 and it was in Roma's stadium, so they had the majority of the support. Phil Neal scored and Prizo scored for them so it was one a piece and, as I've said, Grobbelaar was just fantastic. He put Conti and Graziani off and Joe Fagan asked me before the final penalty if I was alright. I told him I was fine, not realising he was asking me if I was alright to take a penalty. I had to go and take the fifth penalty. The way it worked out, they had missed a couple of penalties, we had missed one through Steve Nicol and it came down to the final penalty. I was bottling it thinking I didn't want to be there - I wanted to be on Star Trek with Scotty beaming me up and taking me away. Then I got my head together, thought of my family and friends and the
people watching and said to myself:
"Whatever you do, don't change your mind."
In the end I changed my mind and it went into the opposite corner that I really wanted to put it! I set off to celebrate and was going to do a cartwheel or a somersault or whatever. In the end I didn't do anything, I just had a little bit of a jump and stamped my feet. The Roma fans started to pelt our fans with bricks and bottles and they pelted our coach as well.
We didn't really get out of the stadium for about three hours, but we went and had a drink and a meal in one of the villas in Rome

and had an absolutely great night. When we got back to Liverpool we had a civic reception and then it was back to the drawing board. I had a great record with Liverpool over seven years - 350 league and cup games, five league championships, four League Cups, three Charity Shields, two European Cups and a couple of caps. I was quite excited about the whole thing.

BERNIE

You got a right rollocking from Bob Paisley during half-time in one game. What was that all about?

ALAN

I wasn't the brightest player ever to sign for Liverpool and had a torrid time in one of my earlier games. I was trying to find Terry McDermott and hit the front men with long balls and forgot to play it short, which is the Liverpool way. Bob came to me first at half-time and it was a good job it wasn't Joe Fagan because he would have killed me. I thought he was going to tell me to knock it short and he came out with:
"They shot the wrong Kennedy in '63."
I thought to myself: "That's a compliment isn't it? Thank you very much boss!" Not realising that he meant if I didn't pull my socks up I would be out.

BERNIE

When you came to the end of your Anfield career were you forced out?

ALAN

It was a combination of my decision, Peter Robinson the secretary and to a certain extent Kenny Dalglish, who was then the manager. He told me I didn't have to go but I felt I was under pressure for my place from Jim Beglin, who was a good eight years younger than me, and that my days were numbered and he was going to be the regular left-back. I had a difficult choicebetween Willie McFaul of Newcastle and Lawrie McMenemy of Sunderland. The deal on offer was exactly the same and Lawrie won my signature because of what he said to me. Willie McFaul was superb and he was gutted that I didn't sign for him. But when I heard what Lawrie was going to do at Sunderland and how he was going to bring them up out of the Second Division, I thought that was the choice to make. He had players there like Eric Gates and Frank Gray and George Burley was about to be signed, so I honestly believed they had the better chance of getting out of the Second Division.

But I failed to realise that Sunderland had lost the first five games of the season, they hadn't got a point and had only scored one goal. When I went there David Hodgson said to me it was great. Unfortunately it didn't work out and of course the manager jumped ship in the 1986-87 season.

BERNIE

Did you play many North East derby games?

ALAN

I didn't, because Newcastle were bottom of the First Division and Sunderland were in the Second Division at the time.

But I played derby games when I was at Newcastle against Sunderland, and of course against Middlesbrough as well. I used to love beating Middlesbrough! We had one great game at Ayresome Park in particular. Middlesbrough were 3-1 up, then I somehow scored with a header from outside the box and Irving Nattrass got the equaliser.

They were great games and I loved them. But fortunately for me I didn't have any encounters with Newcastle while at Sunderland. I left Sunderland after just 18 months of my contract.

BERNIE

After leaving Roker Park you joined a host of other clubs and played until you were nearly 40.

ALAN

I went everywhere - non-league, Hartlepool, Wigan, Colne Dynamoes who were quite a strong and steady non-league side in those days. I went back into league football with Wrexham and finished my professional career with them at the age of 36 due to a knee injury. I was grateful to Kenny Dalglish for letting me train at Liverpool and I went on to play non-league football until I was almost 43 and loved it.
I still play a bit in the Masters tournaments as well.

BERNIE

You gained two full England caps. Should it have been more?

ALAN

It would have been more but for Kenny Sansom, the West Bromwich Albion full-back. He was a decent player and never got injured and he was the real reason I didn't get in the squad. I got in late on under Bobby Robson, who to be fair was very generous to me. There was a time in 1985 when Bobby rang to tell me he was going to have to leave me out of the squad and I was devastated. He said a young centre forward called Gary Linker was replacing me and I told him I understood. The thing

about England at the time - as you know - was they were a bit tight and they put my two caps into one cap.
BERNIE

What have you been up to since retiring?

ALAN

I do a lot of media work at the moment, Champions League stuff. I did a radio show for six years in Manchester called The Legends, the same as you do up here. I did it along with Graeme Sharp - ex-Everton, Mickey Thomas - ex Man United - and Gary Owen, who was at Man City. When I was involved I absolutely loved it, it was a fantastic show and people still ask me why they let it go. It was their decision. Our contracts were up at the end of the season and they told us they wanted to go down different lines. I hope it might get brought back in future. You know what it's like, people just want to talk about their team. Everybody I talk to wants it back on air.

BERNIE

You're still involved with Liverpool on match days. What do you do?

ALAN

I'm the meeter and greeter at the Carlsberg Lounge. They have been the sponsors for the last 20 years. I have been involved for six or seven years. People come in to have a good day. They get the man of the match in after the game - it's usually Torres or Gerrard. We try and give them as good a time as we can so they leave Anfield all excited. John Aldridge and Ian Rush also host lounges as well. It's something I really enjoy doing. We can't all be coaches or managers, but we are all still giving a little

something back to the game. The current players might not give anything back in a few years' time. We run a Liverpool Legends team that goes out on tour every year. Obviously
I have seen you in Singapore playing the games as well.
We love it don't we? We would still rather be playing than talking about it. They say you should always keep playing and that's what I intend to do.

BERNIE

What, if anything, would you say have been the disappointments in your career?

ALAN

Leaving Liverpool was a big disappointment for me personally. When I look back I'd say every time I pulled the red shirt of Liverpool over my head it was an honour. I loved every minute of it. I have settled in the area, although I do go back to the North East quite a bit. I have two wonderful boys and a wife who supports me as I continue to make a living. Life is great at the moment.

Celebrations after winning European Cup yet again!

HONOURS

ALAN PHILIP KENNEDY

PLAYING CAREER HISTORY

1972-1978 Newcastle United
1978-1985 Liverpool
1985-1987 Sunderland
1987   Beerschot
1987   Hartlepool United
1987   Grantham town
1987-1988 Wigan Athletic
1988-1990 Colne Dynamoes
1990-1991 Wrexham

PLAYING HONOURS (winners)

Liverpool

1979,1980,1982,1983,1984 English Championship
1979,1980,1982   Charity shield
1981,1982,1983,1984   League cup
1981,1984   European Cup

CAPS 2 full caps for England

"The truth is there was one person who stood out who had never managed in the Premiership before. The name would have blown us all away, but his agent asked for £11 million a year in salary."

Referring to potential sunderland managers demands.

NIALL QUINN
SUNDERLAND

NIALL
QUINN

Niall John Quinn, or Niall Sean Ocuinn in Irish, was born in 1966 in the fair city of Dublin, Ireland. He played for Arsenal, Manchester City, Sunderland and the Republic of Ireland. He also managed Sunderland for a month.

Quinny became a first team regular at Arsenal in 1986/87 having made his Gunners debut against Liverpool in December 1985. People described him as a tall, gangly, ungainly centre forward with a good touch and an eye for goal. I see similarities between Niall and England centre forward Peter Crouch.

I played against Quinny over the years but we became teammates for the Republic of Ireland.
I've always found Quinny straight-laced, funny and very charismatic. He tells a story about me where I once played an international game wearing a shirt signed by my Republic teammates.

I can only presume he had too much whisky as I can't remember it to this day!
I met up with Niall for a chat while he was playing for Sunderland and have since asked him more up-to-date questions during a couple of his guest appearances on the Three Legends show on Real Radio.

BERNIE

You joined Arsenal straight from the juniors but your first team appearances were limited. Was that due to the strength in depth at Highbury?

QUINNY

I think I got an awful lot very soon. The first or second year I
went there I went from literally playing in the youth team to the
first team overnight. I think I was the same height as I am now,
only three stone lighter. So I wasn't really able to handle myself
that well. I hadn't developed, but I was doing alright. I played
for 18 months and then Alan Smith joined the club and he was a
real quality centre forward, one of the best I've ever seen. I
found it hard obviously trying to displace him and Arsenal were
starting to win titles under George Graham.

I was having bit parts, playing the odd game or two, but I didn't
play when we won the championship. I was at Anfield that night
in the final match of the 1989 season when Michael Thomas
scored and we beat Liverpool to the title. They were great
moments, even though it wasn't the best time in my career. It
was an introduction to top flight football and it was the dream
everyone said it would be. It was tremendous to be at a great
club which created the discipline for being a proper professional
footballer. I think one or two of the lads drank a little too much,
but that was me included maybe. But we learned a lot of good
things and it sets you up for the rest of your career really.

BERNIE

You've played in two World Cup finals. Those must have been
highlights?

QUINNY

I got in late in the 1990 competition in Italy. Tony Cascarino
didn't do that well against Egypt I think it was and Jack
Charlton didn't tell me until an hour before I was due to start
that I was playing. Jack's assistant Maurice Setters hadn't told
me I was going to play in the big match against Holland and he

got a bit of a hammering. It was probably for the best though. Because if he would have told me three days previously I might have spent it worrying too much. I played and it was that great Holland team - Gullit, Van Basten and all of the top men.

BERNIE

And you scored.

QUINNY

I scored. It was one each and it was a great moment, but not as good as when I scored against England at Wembley!

BERNIE

I've worked under big Jack Charlton. How would you describe his style as a manager and as a person?

QUINNY

Jack is incredible. What you see on the pitch and on the training ground is the exact same as you see off it. He's larger than life, he knows exactly what he wants and he gets it, or he wants it in the most peculiar ways possible. Before the World Cup it was all about getting fitness coaches and getting built up to the maximum. We went to Malta pre-season training and it was wet and freezing cold, and he wanted us to get acclimatised.
He made us all put on something like 12 training tops so we were like Michelin men - that was typical of his ideas - to get us ready for the heat in Italy. It was old-fashioned stuff but at the end of the day the method in his madness was brilliant, because it got us such a strong bond and as a group we enjoyed ourselves so much. We were training the same time as Scotland - they had

the bleep test and all the machines going off and we were really the Raggy Arsed Rovers down the other end.

But it was great. That was the kind of thing that got us through but he knew he had world class players and he knew how had to mould them as a team better. Ireland always had great players like Liam Brady and Frank Stapleton, but they never achieved. He just found a way to get us all to bond as a unit and to die for each other. It was the most fabulous thing to be involved with and Jack Charlton was responsible for that. You didn't dare win a game of cards against him either. You would just be about to play the winning card and he would ask you if you wanted to play next week. You would go and put it back and let him win!

BERNIE

Are you aware how much derby games mean, with all of the passion and pride at stake?

QUINNY

Absolutely. My second or third game ever was massive - a derby between Arsenal and Spurs. But the point I would say about that is in London, probably one in 10 people would be bothered about it. In Manchester, I'd say five out of six people are bothered about Man United against Man City. But up here it's 10 out of 10. I mean, every household is interested so much in derbies that it's almost as if the rest of the season doesn't matter.

BERNIE

Do you think Sunderland can beat the quickest-ever derby goal, scored by yours truly after just 17 seconds?

QUINNY

I think I could beat the quickest-ever derby goalscorer in a sprint now, and I'm not very quick! I don't remember the derby goal, you'll have to talk me through it.

BERNIE

Do you get involved in first team affairs in your current role as Sunderland chairman?

QUINNY

No, absolutely not. I get involved in some of the negotiation. But no, Roy (Keane) has full control. He put in a scouting system at Sunderland when he came in and there was only one scout Dave Bowman - a seriously good scout. I look at Dean Whithead, and Nyron Nosworthy and players like that are in our team because of him. Dave left to rejoin Mick McCarthy at Wolves and that was fine, but there was no structure around him. So we had to bring Sunderland into the new era on the scouting side. Dave was great and we now hope we've got 14 Daves all around Europe. I think that Roy learned the Man United way and the results of our youth team would tell you we are doing something right. Kevin Ball and Ged McNamee are doing superb work there.

BERNIE

I believe you are one of the youngest chairmen in the Premier League, if not the youngest. Why haven't you become a manager?

QUINNY

I don't know. Over the last couple of years I was a club captain here and I think Francis Lee once said it of me that I was like a barrack room lawyer. I was always complaining about the way the clubs were being run where I played. I never complained about tactics or got caught up in that.
I didn't do coaching courses and when I came into Sunderland I did feel that things had gone so wrong the year before that we had to kind of hold on and offer some kind of stability.
I put my head on the block, I had no problem with that, and the lads responded magnificently for me.

BERNIE

How difficult was it appointing Roy Keane?

QUINNY

It wasn't difficult at all. When you mentioned his name to the Drumaville consortium, the Irish guys' eyes lit up. There was a couple of others mentioned as well to be truthful. Martin O'Neill was highly sought-after and wasn't working at the time because of his wife's illness. Sam Allardyce is a former captain of the club and those were the names we were thinking about big time. But Roy captured the imagination. He would get the club on the back pages again for the right reasons and because he was young and hadn't done it before he would be given loads of time.
But Roy being Roy, eight months later we got promotion and he surpassed everybody's expectations. The spirit he created around the place - he transformed a team who were nervous and had had a terrible year the year before. The crowd weren't convinced but he turned that bunch of guys around and after Christmas we were turning up to full houses and after 10 minutes we knew we were going to win games.

BERNIE

You tell that story about me playing for the Republic in a shirt signed by all the players. What's that all about?

QUINNY

Bernie, you deny the story but it's absolutely true!
One of our players cried off and in those days you would have 11 players and five subs. And you might have four or five guys - 17, 18 19 and 20 - who would all get a kit but wouldn't be involved. One of our players cried off injured just before one of our World Cup qualifiers started, so you came from the pool of four guys who weren't getting a game. Because you thought you wouldn't be involved you had your tracksuit on. I think you borrowed boots from Noel King, the technical assistant, and when Jack called you on with 10 minutes to go I saw you coming on in this lousy green jersey.
It was all black as well and we were looking at you wondering what was going on and if you had got the jersey signed for a charity. You played a World Cup qualifier with 22 signatures on your jersey!

BERNIE

Quinny, you must have had too much Guinness that day! Since taking over at Sunderland, what's the biggest mistake you've made?

QUINNY

The biggest mistake I've made is getting the guys over the line. I actually drew up a three year budget plan and this was before the new TV deal was announced two years ago, which really blew things out of the water. When I look back on it they must look at me and think I'm some kind of absolute numbwit, because I was so far off the mark. There was an extra zero on to most forecasts and what we would need and where we would need them, what kind of crowd would come and how much people would pay. Forty million pays the wage bill but it doesn't pay anything else - it has doubled or trebled since then.

I think I've had to learn very fast but I'm not ashamed to admit that this monster has grown enormously over this last two years and I've had to really keep concentrating and keep good people around me to keep pace with it all.

BERNIE

Have you still got as much power as chairman since the American owner Ellis Short arrived?

QUINNY

I have as much power, if not more. I've got a great executive team behind me and I have more money. It's no secret the Drumaville guys did what they could and we got it to a new level. But you can trust me with what's happened in the last six to nine months, we've a man who has familiarised himself with the business and doesn't want to make mistakes. We've spoken with Ellis for example on how pleased we were to get our money back on players like Pascal Chimbonda and El-Hadji Diouf. He said: "In future when we sign players, I don't mind giving you a lot more money than we gave you for them. "But don't come to me in four months time and tell me they don't fit in."

BERNIE

When Roy Keane departed you were quoted as saying you had more than 30
managerial candidates and a host of them were world class. Were you telling pork pies?

QUINNY

No, I didn't say world class, I said well-known people in world football. We had four World Cup winners and only three of them had managed before and only one of them could speak English, so they were nowhere near the Premiership. They were all great names, they all brought back great World Cup memories from 12 to 20 years ago and it was amazing to have that.
The point I'm trying to make is Sunderland is known throughout the world, but they didn't have the Premiership experience so that we felt comfortable in offering them the job. The truth is there was one person who stood out who had never managed in the Premiership before. The name would have blown us all away, but his agent asked for £11 million a year in salary.

BERNIE

So are you going to reveal who it was?

QUINNY

No, I don't think so!

BERNIE

How much in total would it cost a Premier League club to be relegated.

QUINNY

I guess from our point of view our generated income in a year would go from
the guts of £70 million to about £27 million. So we would have to work the next year minus £43 million.

BERNIE

Getting knocked out of the FA Cup in the early rounds, what effect does that have on a club financially?

QUINNY

If we didn't make it to the semi-finals, we're not losing anything. A home quarter-final may make a tad of difference, but up until the quarter-finals we wouldn't be losing anything.

BERNIE

I've heard getting knocked out of the fourth round you are set to lose £67,000.

QUINNY

I'm not so sure of the exact figure, but getting knocked out of the FA Cup early doors doesn't hurt us financially.

BERNIE

Is that why managers don't pick the strongest team in the competition?

QUINNY

Well, some do. If you remember last year, Steve Bruce did pick his best side. And to be quite honest about things as they were in January 2011 with the rush of games and the injuries we had, we felt we had enough within the group to dispose of Notts County. It's always easy when you look back, but we had a lot of players playing who hadn't been around for a while, like Andy Reid, and the chemistry and the gel didn't happen. We got ourselves into a bit of trouble and we got one goal back but we didn't get the second. It was a risk that didn't come off.

BERNIE

It's January and the transfer window is open. Are you trying to bring new players to Sunderland?

QUINNY

Well, I think I have to dampen the mood because I'm working harder this time to try and move one or two out to try and pave the way to allow us to bring somebody in. We are carrying a few wages that are hurting the club, particular personnel aren't performing for us week in, week out and that prevents us from doing business. We have done it in the past when we have bought players when we haven't got our squad shape right. Now we just have to be careful because without moving players on and keeping the wages right, I wouldn't be doing my duty properly in protecting the financial strength of the club.

BERNIE

How do you assess the club's progress since you arrived as chairman?

QUINNY

The one thing I would say is we've given ourselves a chance to make the

progress that a club of this stature ought to be making.

It's not about the history, it's all about the future and the longevity. The best way I can describe it to the fans is, we could have attempted to do a Portsmouth or a Leeds United and gone for it at all costs. But that's not going to help this club to increase the probability of it being a yo-yo club.

So we are trying to establish it in such a way that we know we can be a solid top half Premiership club for the next five years, not have one great year and then get relegated.

As a football club we are beginning to get belief right throughout its structure, from the owner, to Steve Bruce, to the fans. There is a bit of belief in the air and sometimes that can be dangerous, but the fans can rest assured that we will not become complacent and we will try our very best to back our belief. It's something that the club deserves.

BERNIE

On occasions you've spoken out against the missing fans. Are you looking for more supporters?

QUINNY

If you want me to set the record straight Bernie, I had a go at the fans who were going to pubs and watching the games illegally.

That's the fans I was having a go at. How can I possibly have a go at the fans that come despite the lack of success at the club? We have won one senior trophy since the war. I can't complain when fans don't come. But when they go to watch it illegally in a pub and spend money supping pints and what have you, then I think I have a right to say: "Hey, you get yourself to the stadium. It will be so much better for the club."

BERNIE

Finally, where do you see Sunderland finishing this season. Are you looking for top 10, Europe? Come on Niall, don't sit on the fence!

QUINNY

Bernie, you're turning into a real media person now, fair play to you! As long as it's the top half.

FOUR days after this interview, Darren Bent left Sunderland to join Aston Villa for £24 million.

HONOURS

NIALL JOHN QUINN

PLAYING CAREER HISTORY

1983-1990 Arsenal
1990-1996 Man City
1996-2002 Sunderland

PLAYING CAREER HONOURS (winners)
Arsenal
1987   League Cup

Sunderland
1999 Division title

1986-2002 Republic of Ireland

MANAGERIAL CAREER HISTORY

2006-   Sunderland

CAPS 92 Full caps for Republic of Ireland.

Niall Quinn MBE.

The mighty Quinn celebrates a goal for the Republic.

As Sunderland manager

"I don't like the phrase 'taking the piss' because that's a bit disrespectful. But we did lord it and showboat a bit."

Referring to a comfortable victory over Newcastle.

GARY ROWELL
SUNDERLAND

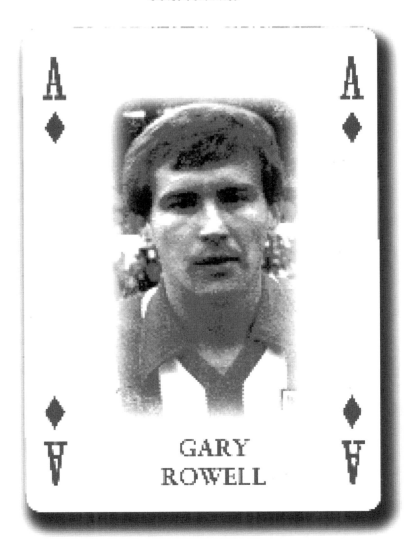

GARY
ROWELL

Gary Rowell was born 6th June 1957. A prolific striker, he joined Sunderland as an apprentice in 1972 and is a cult hero among Black Cats fans who saw him play.

He scored 102 goals for the club and is one of only three players - along with Len Shackleton and Kevin Phillips - to have topped 100 goals for Sunderland since the Second World War.

He wrote his name into Sunderland folklore when he scored a hat-trick against Newcastle United in a 4-1 victory in February 1979, his first career treble.

I played alongside Gary at Middlesbrough when I first arrived in England. I didn't see the best of him as he was nearing the end of his career, but you could still see his qualities.
He was good at holding the ball up, sharp in and around the box and obviously a prolific goalscorer.

At the time I found Gary a fairly quiet family man who enjoyed a laugh. His nickname at Ayresome Park was 'Snatch' and I can assure you it's nothing to do with snatching a goal!
My abiding memory of Gary is from when he was a player at Middlesbrough. Then manager Bruce Rioch would play one against one and two against two in training.
Bruce used to nominate himself nine times out of 10 and would pick Gary as his opponent in a one on one and kick lumps out of him. Gary, to his credit, would return the compliment!

I travelled to the Stadium Of Light to meet up with Gary.

BERNIE

You joined Sunderland straight from school, Gary. That must have been a boyhood dream?

GARY

Absolutely. I was Sunderland-mad from as far back as I can remember, from the age of six or seven. My dad took me to Roker Park and I was hooked from the very first time I went there. It was always my ambition throughout school to play for Sunderland and put the red and white shirt on.

BERNIE

As a Sunderland fan, who were your heroes?

GARY

Pretty much the whole 1973 FA Cup-winning team. I was born in Sunderland and brought up in Seaham, which is just a few minutes outside Sunderland. I was always a Sunderland fan. I was never tempted to follow whoever won the league or FA Cup in a particular year. One of my heroes would have been Micky Horswill, but don't tell him! To be fair, I tell him all the time. I was only 15 when Sunderland won the FA Cup and just loved that team. Winning the FA Cup had such an impact on the town - as it was then. It was absolutely incredible to live through that era, those six months. If you lived through it, you will never forget it. A couple of my king pins were Dennis Tuart and Billy Hughes. They were the flair players of the team, but the whole team were my heroes.

The reason I was so in awe was because I had just joined Sunderland as an apprentice then, so I was part of the club, although no one knew me at the time. We used to train at

289

Washington and the great thing about that team was that the further they got in the cup, it seemed the more relaxed they got. I had one or two heroes before that as well. Charlie Hurley, he is everybody's hero.

BERNIE

What was the background to you joining Sunderland?

GARY

Sunderland were in the Second Division when I signed. There were one or two other clubs after me, but a guy called Charlie Ferguson scouted me for Sunderland. He was a famous name in Sunderland's history. He had scouted loads and loads of the players, and probably half the team that won the cup. I know he got Jim Montgomery and Micky Horswill. Charlie Ferguson was the key talent spotter, if you like. As soon as he asked me to sign for Sunderland, I couldn't ask him for a pen fast enough.

BERNIE

One of your biggest highlights must have been scoring that famous hat-trick in Sunderland's 4-1 demolition of Newcastle at St James' Park?

GARY

It was magnificent. Probably for you it would be the equivalent of scoring a hat-trick against Rangers. Newcastle were our nearest rivals and I had been in the team for a couple of years by then. Just to pull on the red and white shirt against the black and whites is a thrill. For me, it's one of the greatest derbies in the world. There's so much riding on it. Just to play in one was a massive highlight for me, and to get lucky and score three goals was something you daren't even dream about.

BERNIE

Have you still got the match ball?

GARY

I never got it. It was one of those situations after the game where it was the last thing on our minds. As we were getting dressed to go somebody mentioned the match ball, but apparently - and I'm still not really sure if it's true or not - it was the linesman's or referee's last game and it was promised a week before the game to them. I honestly don't know what happened. I never got my hands on it for a minute afterwards. It was never in my possession and to this day I don't know where it is.

BERNIE

You could have got a few quid for it on Ebay!

GARY

No, that would have been sacrilege. The memories are enough and the fans still remember it.
Sunderland and Newcastle games are special and if you do well in them they never let you forget it, and nor would I want them to. I don't need a memento of the ball, although it would have been nice.

BERNIE

On the subject of derbies, do you think they have lost a bit of their sparkle with the influx of foreign players over the years?

GARY

To me, no. Obviously I'm on the outside and I don't know what passion the players show in the dressing room. All I know is I still feel it's the number one game. I don't know about you, but I'm quite relaxed being an ex-player and I don't pine for the days when I used to play football. But if there was one game I could recreate or be part of again, it would be the derby against Newcastle. It still gets me going. I still get butterflies because I always want Sunderland to do well.

BERNIE

Going back to the day you scored the hat-trick, is it true you turned to a couple of your team-mates and asked whether the team should go on to score a fifth or just take the piss?

GARY

We were 4-1 up with 15 minutes to go, and when you're at home that's the longest 15 minutes of your life. You know that they are not going to get back into it. There were sort of words to that effect. We had a free-kick, there was a stoppage in play and we were just bantering amongst ourselves, knowing the game was over and it was pretty much as good as it gets. I don't like the phrase 'taking the piss' because that's a bit disrespectful. But we did lord it and showboat a bit. It's a true story.

BERNIE

Is it true you only missed one penalty in nine or 10 years?

GARY

It was my second one. I vowed I'd never miss another one and luckily I didn't. I think I scored about 21 out of 22.

BERNIE

What was your secret when it came to taking penalties? Was it about power, accuracy, going for the corners, hitting it down the middle?

GARY

I was never someone who lashed it. I always felt that you could still get enough pace on it with your side foot, so I never put my laces through it at all. I always went for accuracy. Sometimes goalies would make your mind up for you. I used to always aim for just inside the post. I used to stay behind in training and practice with Barry Siddall and Chris Turner. I used to say to one of the keepers that I'd take the pealties normally,
then I would tell them which side I was going to put it.
It wasn't a case of being arrogant or anything. My thinking was that if they knew where I was going and I could still stick it in the net, I had a pretty good technique going.
Obviously it's different in training, but I got the confidence to score from the penalty spot even if the keeper sussed out the right way. It was a training drill and a technique that helped me.

BERNIE

Only 11 Sunderland players have scored 100 goals or more for the club and you're one of them.

GARY

It's funny in a way, it sort of crept up on me more than anything. Kevin Phillips was always going to beat my record because he was just an out and out goalscorer. When I started I was a midfielder. It was only in my last three seasons at Sunderland that I was made a striker. For all the rest I was an attacking midfielder. When I first came into the team I was kind of a wide left in a 4-4-2 and I used to love that position. The manager used to give me a fair bit of freedom and I was told to get into the box all the time. That's how I got a nose for goal. Weirdly, I still think of myself as a midfield player. I swear on it. In school I was a midfield player, in the youth team, the reserves and when I first got into the the first team I was always a midfield player. I could always grab a goal and most of the time I was a penalty taker, that helped me. I always felt I accumulated goals rather than bagged goals. I was completely different to Kevin Phillips. I knew he was going to get more than me, unless we sold him and for a while I was hoping we would! To be honest, I wasn't disappointed when he beat my record. I knew it was going to happen and in the end he got 120-odd, he beat me quite comfortably. But I'm happy with my goals. It's a nice thing to look back on and there are only three of us who have done it since the War. Len Shackleton, Kevin Phillips and myself, so I'm in good company.

BERNIE

You never gained a full England cap, despite your fantastic goalscoring record for Sunderland.

GARY

On several occasions I was mentioned or linked periodically and you get your hopes up. It would have been nice, but it didn't happen. It's not something I dwell on or worry about. Maybe I was just a little bit short for that level, I don't know. There were some good strikers around at the time, like Paul Mariner, Tony Woodcock and Trevor Francis. I think back in 1983 I finished with 18 goals in the top flight. Dalglish and Rush probably got a boat load, but there wouldn't have been many English strikers that got more than me that season. Having said that, I am more than happy with the career I had, certainly at Sunderland. That's the club I wanted to play for and that was your bread and butter. Even if you played for England for 10 years, your bread and butter was always your club. In many ways I'm a bigger Sunderland fan than an England fan, although of course you want to go as high as you possibly can.

BERNIE

The Sunderland fans still chant your name this day to the Beatles classic Yellow Submarine. I think that's fantastic.

GARY

It is, it's 25 years since I left Sunderland. I don't think they sing my name because I'm the best player that's ever played for Sunderland. I think the reason they do it - I hope - is because I'm just one of them in many ways. It's often sung at away games when they have got about 4,000 fans. I can still hear them even when I've got the headphones on doing the radio summarising and it gives me such a buzz. I'm forever grateful for everything I've got from the fans and it continues to this day. It's something I love to bits.

BERNIE

Did you ever score in a derby game against Middlesbrough?

GARY

I scored a couple of times against Middlesbrough. Once I got one in from about 40 yards I think after they had to put Peter Brine in goal when the keeper got injured. And once - I've got to get this one in - in a 4-0 win.

BERNIE

Willie Maddren signed you for Middlesbrough for £25,000. Did you have to give it some thought?

GARY

I think you've got to think about every move. But Willie Maddren was a gentleman, probably the nicest guy I've ever met in football. A real honest to goodness bloke. He sold Middlesbrough to me. Obviously coming back to the North East was a big pull and I was really happy to sign. I thought Middlesbrough could go places.

BERNIE

Despite being Boro's leading scorer in your first season, you couldn't prevent relegation to Division Three, when I had just arrived. What was the team lacking at the time?

GARY

There were big problems behind the scenes, as you know, but I wasn't aware of them. I always remember playing Sunderland over Christmas. We beat them 2-0 and I thought we could make a push for promotion. How wrong can you be? January and February came and suddenly from out of nowhere all these problems became apparent. The club had no money, we weren't getting paid and obviously it took a toll. I think ultimately that's why we went down.

BERNIE

Willie was sacked and Bruce Rioch took over. Did you feel it was the right time for a change in management?

GARY

It's hard to say, because when you've got a lot of respect for somebody you don't like to see them go. But perhaps it was. I mean, Willie Maddren was a great servant for Middlesbrough. He brought in players like nobody else on a low budget. There was yourself of course, Pears, Ripley, Pallister, Tony Mowbray. To me, the foundations were there. It was a good team, but I just felt the problems off the field were contributing to why we really struggled. Bruce Rioch came in and it wasn't really his fault at all that Middlesbrough went down. I always felt that the off-field problems contributed to that.

BERNIE

You found yourself out in the cold when Bruce took over. How did you find him as a manager?

GARY

I never got on with him - you know that we used to try to kick each other at training. But, believe it or not, I have got a lot of respect for him. Probably I wouldn't like to invite him for tea and he wouldn't invite me for tea, but the guy captained Scotland and he's had success as a manager, so I respected him like that. But we didn't see eye to eye. It happens in football. The strange thing I'll always remember is me and him trying to kick lumps out of each other in training.

BERNIE

On leaving Middlesbrough you had spells at Brighton, Carlisle and then Burnley. Have you got any regrets?

GARY

I've got loads. There's a lot of people that say they wouldn't change a thing. I would change lots of things. Saying that, when I come to Sunderland I get a really good reception from the supporters and it is sort of my spiritual home. I was at Middlesbrough, I was at other clubs, but I'm a Sunderland boy and I'm a Sunderland fan. I always will be.

BERNIE

What are you doing with yourself these days?

GARY

I'm doing Real Radio, like yourself. We do all the Sunderland games, home and away, and have a phone-in. I do an article in the Wearside Roar monthly fanzine as well. I talk about the current stuff and tell little stories here and there about my playing career, which the fans love to hear I think.
That keeps me in touch with football. I love it.

BERNIE

What games stick out among your 10 years as a summariser?

GARY

It's been a rollercoaster. We have been relegated twice, with the lowest points ever. Beating Newcastle twice sticks out. We beat them 2-1 at St James', then Kieran Richardson laid the ghost of about 30 years to rest. Because when we beat Newcastle at home two years ago, Sunderland hadn't beaten Newcastle on Wearside since 1981, when I played in the team.
That's one of the greatest games in my career. Stan Cummins scored the winner, we beat them 1-0 and we scored at the Sunderland fans' end. It was just absolutely amazing, the noise was incredible. Probably the most bizarre game I have ever seen was when Sunderland lost 3-1 to Charlton and all three goals were own goals. Two of them were scored by the centre forward, Michael Proctor. Just to add a twist to the tale, me and Simon Crabtree, the commentator alongside me, had a first scorer bet on Kevin Phillips. Sunderland were 3-0 down at half-time and Phillips scored a late consolation. The bookies still paid out because own goals didn't count!

BERNIE

Do you enjoy being on the airwaves as much as playing?

GARY

I do look forward to all of the games and enjoy it, but not as much as playing. It's second to putting the shirt on and doing everything that comes with being a professional footballer. But it's a good second. You haven't got the pressure of being a manager and living and dying by results. There is nothing we can do to influence it, but I throughly enjoy it. I am still massively up for the games and even love travelling, to be honest.

BERNIE

Have you ever had any stick from opposing fans?

GARY

I remember when commentator Simon Crabtree went on a bit of a rant after one of the derby games, we received hate mail. We got death threats in fact. Crabbers got more than me to be honest. After one of the derby games when we beat Newcastle at St James', Crabbers went off on a celebration ramble like the commentator did when Norway beat England. He did a version of that including guys like Jimmy Nail, Bobby Robson and Tony Blair, and finished off with the "your boys took a hell of a beating" line. Crabbers got hate mail for quite a while after that and I was roped into it as well, but I always blamed Crabbers!

BERNIE

Since you have retired, who is the best striker you have witnessed at Sunderland?

GARY

Darren Bent was pretty much an out and out goalscorer. Kevin Phillips was the most obsessive goalscorer, if you know what I mean. He really loved scoring goals. As an all-round player, then probably Niall Quinn. Asamoah Gyan could develop, he has got the pedigree and is a World Cup player. I really have high hopes for him.

BERNIE

On the subject of strikers, what did you make of Darren Bent's sudden departure in January 2011?

GARY

People say you shouldn't be shocked by anything in football, but I was totally shocked. He was a guy who was always banging on about how much he loved Sunderland and playing for us. I didn't see it coming at all. But we played hardball and got top dollar for him - £24m from Aston Villa.

BERNIE

Do you have any dealings with the chairman, Niall Quinn?

GARY

No, I tend not to get involved. In fact, I have only got to see him twice in the six years he has been the chairman, and that's only if I bump into him at an away game. He will shake my hand. I think the job we have got in the media, if you get too pally with the club, players or managers it can compromise you a bit. You leave yourself open if anyone says you're biased. Well, I am, but if Sunderland play badly then I will say it.

If there is 40,000 at the game and we have been rubbish, and I'm saying Sunderland were brilliant on air people would be saying "this guy is a joke". I feel you can get too comfortable, so I just try and keep myself to myself.

BERNIE

Have you ever had a fallout with the club over comments you have made?

GARY

No, I don't think so. There was something in the papers years ago, but it was totally bogus. Somebody wrote something accusing me of saying I was asked to leave a press conference. I was actually doing a phone-in at the time, I wasn't even in the press conference.

I can understand why players and managers lose there rag sometimes when the papers print total fabrication. In my case, it was.

HONOURS

GARY ROWELL

PLAYING CAREER HISTORY

1972-1984 Sunderland
1984-1985 Norwich
1985-1986 Middlesbrough
1986-1987 Brighton
1988   Carlisle
1988-1989 Burnley

Roker hot shot Rowell